The Lakeside Company

Thirteen Case Studies in the Life-Cycle of an Audit

Sixth Edition

Joe Ben Hoyle
E. Claireborne Robins School of Business
University of Richmond

John Trussel
Hood College

Richard A. Scott
McIntire School of Commerce
University of Virginia

Prentice Hall
Englewood Cliffs, New Jersey 07632

Project manager: Lynne Breitfeller
Acquisitions editor: Bill Webber
Production coordinator: Ken Clinton

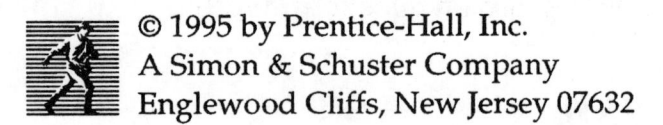

© 1995 by Prentice-Hall, Inc.
A Simon & Schuster Company
Englewood Cliffs, New Jersey 07632

All rights reserved. No part of this book may be
reproduced, in any form or by any means,
without permission in writing from the publisher.

Printed in the United States of America

10 9 8 7 6 5 4 3

ISBN 0-13-289333-9

Prentice-Hall International (UK) Limited, *London*
Prentice-Hall of Australia Pty. Limited, *Sydney*
Prentice-Hall Canada Inc., *Toronto*
Prentice-Hall Hispanoamericana, S.A., *Mexico*
Prentice-Hall of India Private Limited, *New Delhi*
Prentice-Hall of Japan, Inc., *Tokyo*
Simon & Schuster Asia Pte. Ltd., *Singapore*
Editora Prentice-Hall do Brasil, Ltda., *Rio de Janeiro*

CONTENTS

Preface   v

INTRODUCTORY CASE: A Look Inside a CPA Firm   1
Quality control standards/ The engagement team/ advertising by professionals /discussion questions/ written question/ library assignment

CASE 1: Analysis of Potential Audit Client   5
Inquiries by a potential client/ the question of expertise in an unfamiliar industry/ client dispute with incumbent auditors/ sizing up a potential client/ evaluating potential audit problems/ discussion questions/ written questions/ library assignment

CASE 2: New Clients and an Auditor's Legal Liability   11
Peer review and acceptance of clients/ analyzing potential legal liability/ contacting the predecessor auditor and reviewing working papers/ the issue of materiality/ discussion questions/ written questions/ library assignments

CASE 3: Audit Risk and Analytical Procedures   18
Engagement letters/ preliminary audit work/ audit risk model/ inherent risk/ control risk/ planned detection risk/ orientation to the industry and the client/ analytical review techniques/ price competition among CPA firms/ discussion questions/ written questions/ library assignments

CASE 4: Internal Control Structure--Assessing Control Risk   35
Assessing control risk/ preliminary evaluation of the control structure/ documentation of the internal control system--flowcharts, narratives and internal control questionnaires/ discussion questions/ written questions/ library assignment

CASE 5: Tests of Controls   47
Testing details of revenue and cash receipts transactions/ control testing questionnaire for accounts receivable/ confirmation of accounts receivable/ the relationship between the adequacy of the internal control structure and the amount of substantive tests to be performed/ discussion questions/ written questions/ library assignment

CASE 6: Testing the Inventory Procurement System   55
Auditing the purchases and cash disbursements cycle/ broad management assertions/ working paper elements and format/ perpetual inventory system maintained by an outside service organization/ discussion questions/ written question/ library assignment

CASE 7: Designing Substantive Audit Tests   80
The payroll system/ auditing the employee compensation cycle/ profit sharing arrangements/ reviewing a working paper/ discussion questions/ written questions/ library assignment

CASE 8: Observation of Physical Inventory Count   88
Taking and observing inventory counts/ cut-off tests/ audit program for substantive tests of inventory/ discussion questions/ written questions

CASE 9: Resolving Audit Problems   100
Warehouse expansion and renovation/ financing the expansion/ interest capitalization/ repairs and maintenance analysis/ leasing a store from a related party/ uncertainty regarding the continued existence of an owned store/ discussion questions/ written questions/ library assignment

CASE 10: Review of Subsequent Events   114
Subsequent events considered/ concluding the audit/ estimating liability for product warranty/ discussion questions/ written questions/ library assignment

CASE 11: Sampling for Attributes   122
Selecting the attributes to test/ setting the acceptable risk of overreliance and the tolerable exception rate/ determining the estimated population exception rate/ calculating the sample size/ evaluating the results of attributes sampling/ discussion questions/ written questions/ library assignment

CASE 12: Sampling for Variables--Difference Estimation   131
Choosing the statistical method/ setting acceptable risk levels and tolerable misstatement/ estimating standard deviation/ calculating sample size/ evaluating sample results/ calculating precision interval/ discussion questions/ written questions

CASE 13: Advisory Services   145
Letter of recommendations to management/ control structure deficiencies/ proposal to update the computer-based accounting system/ discussion questions/ written questions/ library assignment

PREFACE

The Lakeside Company was conceived in 1980 as a means of introducing students to the world of auditing that exists outside of a college textbook. Since that time, these cases have been used at hundreds of universities by thousands of students. The current edition is the fourth reiteration of the idea that was first formed back in 1980. Over the years, these cases have evolved to mirror both the continual changes found in the auditing profession as well as refinements in our approach to the presentation of many subjects. In this edition, we have updated all of the material, rewritten most of the cases, improved the computer assignments, rearranged the ordering of several cases, and included additional library assignments. We believe this fourth edition is a particularly efficient and effective educational tool.

Few courses at any college are more interconnected with actual practice than Auditing. Many accounting majors find themselves serving as a member of a real audit team within just a few months following graduation. Textbooks have traditionally approached the subject by attempting to develop an appreciation in students for the various aspects of an audit: client acceptance, potential legal liabilities, internal control evaluation, audit risks, analytical procedures, and the like. Although each of these topics can be comprehended in the abstract, understanding is frequently enhanced if students can place them within the context of an actual audit. Unfortunately, most college students do not have the opportunity to participate in an audit experience prior to graduation.

The cases in The Lakeside Company are intended to create a realistic view of how an auditor organizes and carries out an audit examination. These cases provide a simulation that permits students to put the abstract and difficult concepts of auditing into practice. Students are guided through the life cycle of an audit, from beginning to end. Every effort has been made to provide situations that are not particularly unusual, the kinds of problems that an auditor might face each day on the job.

Students are introduced to a world where decisions must be made under conditions of risk and uncertainty, client pressures, and time restraints. Although these cases cover the diverse components of an audit, their main focus is on assisting students to develop an understanding of the logic used by auditors in making a determination about a client's financial statements.

In contrast to most accounting textbooks, the questions and concerns posed by these cases rarely have set answers that are ultimately correct. We believe that in a real audit no easy answers usually exist for the many complex problems that may be encountered. Instead, the auditor must analyze each situation, consult with authoritative literature, and finally rely on personal judgement to justify the actions being taken. Students simply looking for answers and procedures to memorize may be frustrated by The Lakeside Company. Conversely, students who question what they are told, refuse to accept untested assertions, and enjoy the interchange of ideas about the real meaning of events, actions, and figures are often fascinated by these cases.

When The Lakeside Company was first developed, we wanted to create a tool that was readily adaptable to the needs of any college professor. Therefore, several characteristics of these cases should be noted:

1. The cases can be used with any textbook. Students should consult frequently with their textbooks to help them resolve difficulties and justify their actions but the cases are not dependent on the use of any particular book.

2. The cases can be used in virtually any order; each one is written as a relatively independent situation. Where time is a problem, some cases may simply be omitted. Obviously, not all professors want to approach this course in a predescribed manner. The Lakeside Company cases can be ordered in any way that best fits each professor's preferred presentation.

3. The cases offer an array of possible approaches: discussion questions, written questions, computer assignments, and library assignments. The type of questions can be used that suits a particular professor's style. These cases were originally intended for open classroom discussion, many times like a debate. However, professors may opt to use only the written, computer or library assignments or some combination.

4. Students can work individually or in teams. One possibility is to divide the class into audit teams at the beginning of the semester so that the students can experience working in groups, a skill that is essential in auditing.

5. The Lakeside Company is based on a regional, public accounting firm as well as a regional, nonpublic business client. Virtually all of the questions, though, relate equally to both smaller and larger firms and clients.

6. For the instructor, there is a supplemental manual providing complete, detailed solutions to all discussion questions and written questions.

7. For the student, there is a software package that includes word processing and spreadsheet templates that may be used to solve many

of the written questions. These questions are indicated by the notation "(DISK: CASE#.DOC)" for generic word processing templates, and by the notation "(DISK: CASE#.WKS)" for spreadsheet templates. Also available on this package is a menu-driven spreadsheet by the name of "TIME.WKS" that will allow students to keep a record of the time they spent on each case, or segment of a case. An estimated time budget is also included so that comparisons may be made to the time actually taken. Perhaps a sense of the importance of time and service being rendered will be impressed upon the student if they are asked to keep track of the time actually spent. No special instructions are needed to use the time report. Upon adoption, master disks of this package are available to instructors for classroom or laboratory use. In the event that this book was purchased for self-study, a copy of the master disk can be obtained by contacting Patti Dant at 800-227-1816.

We hope that you find your experiences with The Lakeside Company to be both educational and enjoyable. Auditing is truly a fascinating subject to study. We have tried to capture some of our enthusiasm for this topic within these cases. The emotional approach to education is often dependent on one's perspective. For example, is determining the areas within an audit of high inherent risk drudgery or an interesting exploration of a client company? Is estimating a warranty liability a boring mechanical procedure or a type of puzzle where all available information must be sorted through to arrive at a viable estimation of a future event? Ultimately, each student must decide whether the material is to be viewed as interesting or dull. We hope these cases will share some of our interest in auditing.

We would like to thank the reviewers of the 3rd edition of The Lakeside Company who provided us with numerous suggestions and ideas for improvement:

Robert J. Koester
Professor
California State University
Dominguez Hills

Colleen O'Keefe
Manager
Arthur Andersen & Co.
Richmond, Virginia

Best wishes for a great class!

Joe Hoyle
John Trussel
Richard Scott

"The real purpose of books is to trap the mind into doing its own thinking."

Christopher Morley

INTRODUCTORY CASE

A LOOK INSIDE A CPA FIRM

The CPA firm of Abernethy and Chapman is located in the central portion of Virginia. This partnership began operations in 1969 and now employs 145 accountants out of a main office in Richmond and three branches in nearby Virginia cities. The Richmond office has 87 professionals: 10 partners, 14 managers, 21 senior and 42 staff auditors. Eleven members of this group concentrate in tax consultation while another seven offer a variety of advisory services to the firm's clients. The remainder spend a majority of their time performing audits and related activities. During busy periods, individuals occasionally have to move from one area of the firm to another. An additional eighteen employees comprise the secretarial and clerical staff of the Richmond office.

In hiring professionals, the firm considers only college graduates with a major in accounting and requires that each employee sit for the C.P.A. exam within one year of employment. Once employed, all accountants in the firm must complete at least 40 hours per year of continuing education. Promotions within the firm are guided by seniority and technical competence. For example, for a staff auditor to be promoted to senior auditor, he or she must have been with the firm at least two years and must have demonstrated outstanding competence in job performance.

Quality control standards and employee policies of the firm are monitored by Heather Axelson, a partner in the Richmond office. One of Ms. Axelson's responsibilities is to conduct training seminars for new professionals regarding the policies of the firm. Under these policies, employees must sever all financial ties to audit clients. Another of Ms. Axelson's duties is to assign personnel to the various audit engagements of the firm. In making these assignments, she considers the employee's experience with the client's business, as well as his or her technical training. For audit engagements, firm policy requires the assignment of a consulting partner, as well as a partner-in-charge of the engagement. The partner-in-charge of the audit heads the engagement team, while the consulting partner advises and reviews the final work of the team.

The engagement team consists of a partner-in-charge, a manager, a senior auditor, and one or more staff auditors. The partner-in-charge of the engagement has the definitive responsibility for decisions made during the audit, even though he or she does not normally carry out the major activities of the audit. The manager, senior auditor and staff auditors perform the majority of the procedures required by an audit. The assignment of an engagement team, as well as a consulting partner, is to ensure not only that audits are appropriately supervised but also that there is complete objectivity and competence in conducting each audit.

Abernethy and Chapman as a firm, and the Richmond office in particular, has experienced considerable growth over the past five years. The partners believe that the increase in revenues has been generated by a good marketing strategy and a continuing emphasis on high-quality auditing and accounting services. During the most recent fiscal year, the Richmond office totalled over $2,500,000 in gross revenues while earning nearly $900,000 in net income. Profits accruing to individual partners ranged from $65,000 to $200,000. Traditionally, 60% of the firm's income has been derived from audit engagements with tax services providing another 25% of the total. Remaining revenues are generated by attestation functions other than audits (e.g., reviews), accounting and bookkeeping services (e.g., compilations) and management advisory services. The partners have agreed that the audit function offers the greatest potential for expanding the firm's income and have constantly stressed the growth of this service.

At present, Abernethy and Chapman has a number of large clients in the Richmond area: a small hotel chain, a group of furniture stores, several large car dealerships, and three of the local banks. Recently, the firm decided to seek additional clients, especially in the audit area. Therefore, within the last 18 months, a series of advertisements has been published in local newspapers as well as in several prominent Virginia periodicals. In addition, a monthly newsletter describing current accounting and taxation changes is distributed to clients and local business leaders. This marketing strategy was created by a Richmond advertising agency and has stressed the theme "We Are Here To Help Your Business." The entire campaign cost the firm $53,000 and has just recently begun to generate additional revenues.

DISCUSSION QUESTIONS

Note to students: Many of the questions in this book are open-ended, designed to stimulate your ability to analyze auditing problems. Often, as in a real audit, no absolutely correct answer is possible. You must evaluate the facts and attempt to arrive at a logical conclusion or a viable course of action. To guide your analysis, you may want to consult a standard auditing textbook, the "Statements on Auditing Standards" issued by the Auditing Standards Board, or any other relevant authoritative pronouncements produced by the AICPA.

(1) What are the main duties of each of the positions that comprise Abernethy and Chapman's engagement team (i.e., partner-in-charge, manager, senior auditor and staff auditor)?

(2) What is the purpose of having both a partner-in-charge and a consulting partner on each audit engagement?

(3) Can an accounting firm hope to accrue any real benefits from a marketing campaign such as the one carried out by Abernethy and Chapman? Should the management of a company select its auditors based on advertisements?

(4) In recent years, many CPA firms have been acquired by larger (often national or international) firms. Why might a large organization consider purchasing an accounting firm such as Abernethy and Chapman? Why might Abernethy and Chapman agree to be acquired? Is this "merger mania" good for the auditing profession?

WRITTEN QUESTION

(1) You have been asked to review the quality control standards of Abernethy and Chapman. Prepare a memo to Ms. Axelson addressing the firm's policies. Be sure to consider all of the elements of quality control as recommended by the Quality Control Standards Committee of the AICPA (i.e., independence, assigning personnel to engagements, consultation, supervision, hiring, professional development, advancement, acceptance and continuation of clients, and inspection).

LIBRARY ASSIGNMENT

(1) Read the following as well as any other published information concerning the advertising of public accounting firms:

"Advertising and Marketing: Should You and How," Practical Accountant, March, 1985, p. 49.
"Advertising: A Professional Controversy," The Ohio CPA Journal, Autumn, 1985, p. 21.
"CPA Advertising: How Successful Has It Been?" Financial Executive, September, 1984, p. 34.
"Advertising - In The Public Interest?" Journal of Accountancy, January, 1984, p. 59.
"The Changing Face of Accounting Advertising," Journal of Professional Services Marketing, 1991, p. 113.
"Accounting for Marketing Success," Journal of Accountancy, March, 1993, p. 44.
"Tracking a Firm's Marketing Achievements," Journal of Accountancy, July, 1992, p. 60.

Write a report discussing advertising by public accounting firms. Indicate the reasons that advertising is permitted and the type of advertising that has occurred. Discuss the success that firms have achieved and the reaction of accountants to this form of marketing. In addition, describe the possible problems that can occur.

CASE 1

ANALYSIS OF POTENTIAL AUDIT CLIENT

Benjamin M. Rogers is the president of the Lakeside Company, a retailer and distributor of audio equipment based in Richmond, Virginia. Although Lakeside had previously been audited by King and Company CPAs, another Richmond firm, Rogers has recently become aware of Abernethy and Chapman from reading several advertisements. His interest in the firm was heightened when he discovered that Abernethy and Chapman audited the primary bank with which he did business. During March of 1994, Rogers contacted his banker who arranged for the businessman to have lunch with one of the CPA firm's partners. At that time, a wide-ranging conversation was held concerning Lakeside as well as Abernethy and Chapman. Rogers discussed the history of the audio equipment company along with his hopes for the future. The partner, in turn, described many of the attributes possessed by his public accounting firm. Subsequently, Rogers requested a formal appointment with Richard Abernethy, the managing partner of Abernethy and Chapman, in hopes of arriving at a final conclusion concerning Lakeside's 1994 audit engagement.

A June 1 meeting was held at the accounting firm's Richmond office and was attended by Abernethy, Rogers, and Wallace Andrews, an audit manager with the CPA firm who would be assisting in the investigation of this prospective client. Both auditors were quite interested in learning as much as possible about the audio equipment business. Although a number of similar operations are located in the Richmond area, Abernethy and Chapman has never had a client in this field. Thus, the Lakeside engagement offers an excellent opportunity to break into a new market.

During a rather lengthy conversation with Rogers, Abernethy and Andrews were able to obtain a significant quantity of data about the Lakeside Company and the possible audit engagement. Included in this information were the following facts:

* Rogers originally began Lakeside in 1977 as a single store that sold radios, televisions, and stereo equipment. This business did well and the company expanded thereafter at the rate of one new store every two or three years. Presently six stores are in operation, three in Richmond with one in each of three nearby cities: Charlottesville, Fredericksburg, and Petersburg. The first five were set up in rented spaces within small shopping centers. However, the most recent store was located in a building constructed by Lakeside itself, adjacent to a new shopping mall on the east side of Richmond. In addition, Lakeside owns a warehouse which also provides office space for the company's

administrative staff.

* In 1987, the marketing of televisions was dropped by Lakeside in a move to concentrate on the sale of radios and, especially, audio equipment. At about the same time, Lakeside became the sole distributor of Cypress Products for the states of Virginia and North Carolina. Cypress is the manufacturer of a quality line of audio equipment. Shortly there-after, the Lakeside stores began to carry Cypress products almost exclusively. Despite the quality of Cypress equipment, the brand was not well known in the Richmond area and store revenues began to decline. Sales did rebound somewhat in 1992 and 1993, although Rogers admitted to Abernethy that all of the stores had suffered from intense competition within the local market. He even indicated that a small audio equipment company, consisting of two stores, had gone bankrupt in Richmond during the past six months. However, he was not certain as to the specific cause of that failure.

* To market the Cypress brand across the states of Virginia and North Carolina, Lakeside hired a staff of six sales representatives who visit audio, electronics, and appliance stores. These retailers could then order merchandise by telephoning the Richmond headquarters/warehouse. After a credit check, requested inventory is shipped to these customers and billed at 2/10; n/45. Up to 20% of the merchandise can be returned to Lakeside within four months as long as the goods have not been damaged. In the past, returns have been low. Rogers indicated that distributorship sales had initially been disappointing but had risen materially in the last two years as the Cypress reputation began to spread.

* Audio equipment inventory is purchased periodically from Cypress. Regional distributors such as Lakeside are allowed 90 day terms but Cypress encourages quick payment by offering large cash discounts. In hopes of maintaining a high profit margin, Rogers has chosen to take all available discounts. To meet the payment terms, Lakeside holds bank credit lines with two Richmond banks totalling $750,000. Interest on this debt is based on the floating prime rate of the respective banks and has averaged just 6%-8% during recent years. Both banks require that cash in an amount equal to 5% of the outstanding credit line remain on deposit.

* The company's warehouse, as well as the sixth store, were constructed with funds provided by loans from the National Insurance Company of Virginia. The first of these obligations was obtained at a 9 1/4% annual interest rate while the second holds a rate of 10%.

* Rogers stated that he was quite unhappy with the services of his present CPA firm, King and Company. He enumerated three grievances that he had with that organization. First, he felt the firm had provided little assistance in updating Lakeside's accounting systems. Lakeside was simply outgrowing the control features of its current systems and, Rogers asserted, King and Company had not provided the needed input for upgrading them. Second, Rogers believed that King and Company was charging an excessive fee for its annual audit. He stated that he was no longer willing to pay that much money for, what he termed were, inferior services.

* Rogers' final problem with King and Company revolved around the audit opinion that was rendered on Lakeside's financial statements for the year ending December 31, 1993. An additional paragraph was added by the auditors to draw attention to an uncertainty. King and Company was not satisfied that the company would be able to recover the $186,000 investment in its latest store. This sixth store, which opened in November of 1992, was constructed adjacent to a shopping center that had proven to be very unsuccessful. To date, the shopping center had leased less than 40% of its available space. The Lakeside store had, consequently, never been able to generate the customer traffic necessary to even come close to a break-even point. The continuing failure of the shopping center made the fate of the Lakeside store appear quite uncertain to King and Company.

* Lakeside Company is owned by a group of eight investors. Rogers (who is 46 years old) owns 30% of the outstanding stock while the remaining seven stockholders individually possess between 6% and 22% of the company's shares. Although all of the investors live in the Richmond area, only Rogers is involved actively in the day-to-day operations of the business. The Board of Directors is comprised of Rogers, two other owners, and a local lawyer. When the company was first organized, all eight shareholders agreed that an audit by an independent CPA firm would be held annually. This same requirement was also a stipulation made by the banks participating in Lakeside's financing.

* Each of the six stores is operated by a manager and an assistant manager. Normally, three to six sales clerks also work at each outlet on a part-time basis. In hopes of stimulating lagging store sales, Rogers initiated a bonus system during 1993 which already appears to be boosting revenues. Under this plan, every manager and assistant manager will receive a cash bonus each January based on the income earned by their store during the previous year. The bonus figure is a percentage of the gross profit of the store less any directly allocable expenses.

* Lakeside Company is in the process of opening a new store which will begin operations by December of 1994. Earlier this year Rogers formed his own separate corporation to construct this latest facility. Upon completion, the building will be leased to Lakeside for its entire life. Although Rogers was confident that this new store would do well, he wanted to avoid any further accounting problems associated with the uncertainty of success.

* Rogers indicated to Abernethy that growth was one of his primary business objectives. He stated that the Cypress distributorship offered unlimited opportunity and that, once firmly established, each of the Lakeside stores was a sound financial investment.

DISCUSSION QUESTIONS

(1) Why would the owners of Lakeside as well as the company's banks require that an annual audit be made by an independent CPA firm?

(2) This case implies that no auditor with the firm of Abernethy and Chapman has an in-depth understanding of the audio equipment business. Is a CPA firm allowed to accept an engagement without having established the necessary expertise to oversee the audit? Would the knowledge required to audit an audio equipment company differ significantly from that needed in the examination of a car dealership?

(3) Many businesses encounter significant uncertainties yet most opinions do not include an extra "explanatory" paragraph. Why did Lakeside's problem with its store number six lead the auditors to provide the additional warning? What other uncertainties might cause an auditor to include an explanatory paragraph?

(4) Lakeside has recently created a profit-sharing bonus plan. Why might such an incentive be a special concern to an auditor?

(5) Rogers wants Abernethy and Chapman to assist his company in developing new accounting systems. Does a CPA firm face an independence problem in auditing the output of systems that its own employees have designed and installed?

(6) Andrews was also assigned to visit the headquarters/warehouse of Lakeside to tour the facility. What should Andrews observe, and what factors should he be especially aware of during this visit?

WRITTEN QUESTIONS

(1) Following the above conference with Rogers, Abernethy asks Andrews to produce a memo listing the potential problems that the firm might encounter in this audit. Prepare this memo for the Lakeside engagement. Include all accounts and transactions that seem to require special attention. Evaluate the possible severity of each of these concerns.

(2) Prepare the auditor's report that King and Company rendered at the end of the 1993 engagement. How does this opinion differ from a standard auditor's report? (DISK: CASE1.DOC)

LIBRARY ASSIGNMENT

(1) Read the following as well as any other published information concerning auditor changes by companies:

"An Analysis of the Economic Factors Related to Auditor-Client Disagreements Preceding Auditor Changes," Auditing: A Journal of Practice and Theory, Fall, 1993, p. 1.
"Corporate Takeovers and Auditor Switching," Auditing: A Journal of Practice and Theory, Spring, 1993, p. 65.
"Shopping Around: A Closer Look at Opinion Shopping," Journal of Accountancy, April, 1986, p. 120.
"Switching Independent Auditors: An Empirical Investigation," Akron Business and Economic Review, Summer, 1991, p. 173.
"The Potential Determinants of Auditor Change," Journal of Business Finance & Accounting, Summer, 1988, p. 243.

The periodic selection of a new auditing firm by a company is not an uncommon practice. Write a report discussing auditor changes. Why do companies change auditors? What kinds of disclosures are required when a company changes auditors? Are companies merely "shopping around" for the audit opinion they desire? Does this seem ethical to you?

CASE 2

NEW CLIENTS AND AN AUDITOR'S LEGAL LIABILITY

During August of 1992, the Virginia-based CPA firm of Abernethy and Chapman underwent a peer review of its quality control procedures. Although the final report of the outside review team was quite laudatory, it did criticize the lack of control demonstrated in accepting new audit engagements. Until that time, this decision was left solely to the managing partner who often made little or no investigation of a potential client before committing the firm's services. The review team pointed out that this policy failed to protect the firm against becoming involved in engagements with undesirable clients.

Following the peer review, Abernethy and Chapman created a three-partner committee to screen each potential client. This group was empowered to make the ultimate decision as to whether the firm should actively seek a particular audit. Under guidelines established by this committee, a partner was put in charge of researching any possible new engagement. This partner had to complete several forms and provide other data describing every potential client. The partner also had to attach a final recommendation letter evaluating the wisdom of seeking the audit. The committee would then review all of this documentation and instruct the partner as to the appropriate course of action.

Two of the documents required for each new engagement were an "Analysis of Potential Legal Liability" and "Information from Predecessor Auditor" (presented in Exhibits 2-1 and 2-2). Before completing these forms, the in-charge partner learns as much as possible about the potential client and its industry. For example, either the partner or a member of the audit staff reviews recent annual reports and tax returns, tours the company facilities, reads any applicable AICPA Industry Audit Guides, and talks with the business references furnished by the possible client. In addition, the partner always discusses the new engagement with the company's previous auditors.

In investigating the Lakeside Company, Richard Abernethy was aware that much might be learned from a conference with the predecessor CPA firm, King and Company. Because of the confidential nature of audit information, arrangements for this discussion were made through Benjamin Rogers, president of Lakeside. An appointment was scheduled for June 15, 1994 so that Abernethy could talk with William King, the managing partner of King and Company.

At this meeting, King did not appear to be surprised that the Lakeside Company was seeking a new independent auditing firm. He talked quite candidly with Abernethy about the engagement. "I assumed when we added the uncertainty wording to our 1993 opinion that it would be our last year on the job. Rogers is really interested in stimulating growth and becoming president of a large company. I am positive that he did not like taking an uncertainty problem to his stockholders or to the banks that finance his inventory. That could scare them and put a damper on his expansion.

"I was comfortable working with Rogers. He, as well as all of the members of his organization, appear to be people of integrity. However, he was always unhappy with our fees. I honestly don't believe that he understands the purpose of an audit or all of the work that the job entails.

"I must admit that Rogers argued vehemently against the uncertainty warning. He based his arguments on two points: first, that no real uncertainty existed, and second, that even if Store Six represented an uncertainty, the potential loss was not material. As to the uncertainty, our firm was never able to satisfy itself that Lakeside was not going to be stuck holding a totally worthless building in a failed shopping center. Rogers simply disagreed; he could only see the most optimistic possibilities for that store. Unfortunately, the materiality question was even more complex. The company had invested approximately $186,000 in that store out of $1.8 million in total assets. Rogers contended that, at the very worse, he could sell the building for $50,000 - $75,000. Of course, that's all in his crystal ball. With the company having a net worth of less than $500,000, our partners felt that an added paragraph to describe the uncertainty was absolutely necessary. We didn't want everyone blaming us if he had to take a $186,000 write off next year.

"The company's situation is really quite unique. The audio equipment stores are only marginal operations. Rogers ruined them when he turned them into Cypress outlets. The market in the Richmond area is just not strong enough for that particular brand alone. On the other hand, he has done exceptionally well with the distributorship side of the business. Across Virginia and North Carolina a very large potential demand seems to have developed for Cypress products. Rogers is just now beginning to tap into that market. Consequently, he is trying to operate one stagnant and one prospering business at the same time. I certainly foresee the distributorship sales growing rapidly over the next few years. I will be interested in seeing how well the internal systems of the company are able to adapt to that expansion, especially since Rogers dislikes spending any money."

Before ending the conversation, King assured Abernethy that the working papers of past examinations would be available for review if Abernethy and Chapman were retained to do Lakeside's current audit. The working papers consisted of a permanent file of information gathered about Lakeside and annual working paper files containing all of the evidence accumulated during each of the previous yearly examinations.

DISCUSSION QUESTIONS

(1) King and Company faced a materiality question in forming its 1993 audit opinion. How do auditors evaluate the materiality of an item in a specific engagement? Do you believe that the investment in the sixth store was actually material to the Lakeside Company?

(2) When a major uncertainty exists, the reporting entity must fully disclose all relevant information within its financial statements. Some auditors believe that this disclosure fulfills the reporting requirements; thus, an explanatory paragraph within the audit report provides no additional information to the reader and is neither beneficial nor needed. Why is uncertainty disclosure still considered necessary by the auditing profession? Should this requirement be dropped or changed?

(3) If Rogers had not consented in having Abernethy talk with the predecessor auditor, what actions would have been open to Abernethy?

(4) If Abernethy had learned from King that Rogers or his staff lacked integrity, what action should have then been followed and why?

(5) What is the purpose of a peer (quality) review? Why have peer reviews become necessary? What does the peer review team examine?

(6) What is the purpose of working papers and what general data should be found in (1) a permanent file and (2) an annual working paper file?

(7) King mentioned that Rogers did not fully comprehend the purpose of an audit. What obligation does a CPA firm have to ensure that a client understands the audit function?

(8) Rogers apparently does not like paying for an audit. Should Abernethy suggest that a review rather than an audit be made of Lakeside's financial statements? What is the difference between a review and an audit?

(9) Richard Abernethy has to make a recommendation to the partner review committee as to whether the CPA firm should seek the audit engagement of the Lakeside Company. If you were Abernethy, what would you recommend?

WRITTEN QUESTIONS

(1) Exhibits 2-1 and 2-2 are attached. From the information that has been presented in the first two cases, complete these forms. (DISK: CASE2.DOC)

(2) If the firm of Abernethy and Chapman does seek and receive this audit engagement, a review will be made of the working papers produced by the predecessor auditor. Prepare a list of the specific contents that should be examined. Indicate each area that should be reviewed and the purpose of studying these particular working papers.

(3) Assume that Abernethy and Chapman audits Lakeside's 1994 financial statements and gathers sufficient, competent evidence to render an unqualified opinion without any mention of the uncertainty. Assume further that Lakeside opts to issue comparative statements showing figures for 1993 and 1994. Write a single audit report that will inform the reader of both opinions as well as the examination made by the previous auditors.

LIBRARY ASSIGNMENTS

(1) Read the following as well as any other published information concerning the peer review of public accounting firms:

"Arranging For A Successful Review," Journal of Accountancy, December, 1989, p. 72.
"The CPA Gets Audited," The Woman CPA, October, 1989, p. 20.
"How Three Firms Benefited From Peer Review," Journal of Accountancy, June, 1989, p. 87.
"Lessons Learned From Peer Review," Journal of Accountancy, April, 1989, p. 96.
"Preparing For Quality Review," The CPA Journal, December, 1988, p. 24.
"A Firm's Experience with Quality Review," CPA Journal, May, 1991, p. 74.
"Standards for Performing and Reporting on Quality Reviews," Journal of Accountancy, March, 1994, p. 94.

Write a report describing the purpose of a peer review. Discuss the reasons that peer reviews have become necessary and the type of examination that is performed.

(2) Read the following as well as any other published information concerning materiality in an audit examination:

"A Comparison of Various Materiality Rules of Thumb," The CPA Journal, June, 1989, p. 62.
"Welcome Guidance on Materiality and Audit Risk," CA Magazine, November, 1988, p. 65.
"Planning Materiality and SAS No. 47," Journal of Accountancy, December, 1987, p. 72.
"How to Evaluate Audit Risk and Materiality," Practical Accountant, October, 1987, p. 74.
"Materiality--How Applied?" The CPA Journal, November, 1986, p. 114.
"An Inventory of Materiality Guidelines in Accounting Literature," CPA Journal, July, 1990, p. 50.
"Materiality: An Inter-Industry Comparison of the Magnitudes and Stabilities of Various Quantitative Measures," Accounting Horizons, December, 1989, p. 71.

In Case 2, King and Company had to make a decision as to the materiality of a potential problem. Write a report describing the methods used by auditors in making this type of judgment.

(3) Read the following as well as any other published information concerning the accountant's legal liability:

"Legal Liability is Having a Chilling Effect on the Auditor's Role," Accounting Horizons, June, 1993, p. 82.
"The Liability Crisis in the U.S. and Its Impact on Accounting," Accounting Horizons, June, 1993, p. 88.
"Accountants' Legal Liability: A Crisis that Must be Addressed," Accounting Horizons, June, 1993, p. 92.
"Accountants' Liability: Coping with the Stampede to the Courtroom," Journal of Accountancy, September, 1987, p. 118.
"Professional Liability: The Situation Worsens," Journal of Accountancy, November, 1985, p. 57.

The auditor's exposure to law suits has been increasing over the last few decades. Write a report describing the profession's exposure to legal liability. Why has the auditors exposure to liability been increasing? What has the profession done to deal with this situation?

Exhibit 2-1

Abernethy and Chapman

ANALYSIS OF POTENTIAL LEGAL LIABILITY

Potential Client: _____

Type of Engagement: _____

Form Completed By: _____ Date: _____

(1) Is the potential client privately-held or publicly-held?

(2) Evaluate the possible liability to the client that Abernethy and Chapman might incur, if the engagement is accepted.

(3) List the third parties that presently have a financial association with the potential client and could be expected to see the financial statements.

(4) Discuss the possibility that other third parties will be brought into a position where they would be expected to see the financial statements of the potential client.

(5) Evaluate the possible liability to third parties, both present and potential, that Abernethy and Chapman might incur if the engagement is accepted.

Exhibit 2-2

Abernethy and Chapman

INFORMATION FROM PREDECESSOR AUDITOR

Potential Client: _____

Form Completed By: _____

Predecessor Auditor: _____

Date of Interview: _____

(1) Discuss the predecessor auditor's evaluation of the integrity of the management of the potential client.

(2) Did the predecessor auditor reveal any disagreements with management as to accounting principles, auditing procedures, or other similarly significant matters? If so, fully describe these disagreements.

(3) What was the predecessor auditor's understanding as to the reasons for the change in auditors?

(4) Did the predecessor auditor give any indication of other significant audit problems associated with the potential client?

(5) Did the predecessor auditor indicate any problem in allowing Abernethy and Chapman to review prior years' working papers for the potential client? If "yes," explain.

(6) Was the predecessor auditor's response limited in any way?

CASE 3

AUDIT RISK AND ANALYTICAL PROCEDURES

On June 28, 1994, Richard Abernethy, managing partner of Abernethy and Chapman, met with the firm's three-member engagement review committee to discuss the Lakeside Company audit. Although Abernethy admitted that the job had some problems, he strongly recommended seeking Lakeside as an audit client. He described Lakeside as an established Richmond company with an almost unlimited growth potential through the distributorship side of its business. Furthermore, he believed that the engagement offered an excellent opportunity for Abernethy and Chapman to gain entry into a new audit area: audio equipment.

Abernethy indicated that he had talked with King and Company, the predecessor auditors. Abernethy not only described the controversy that had arisen over the auditor's 1993 uncertainty opinion but also indicated that King and Company appeared to have no reservations about the integrity of Lakeside's management. In addition, if retained, Abernethy and Chapman would be allowed to review the prior years' audit working papers. Wallace Andrews, an audit manager with Abernethy and Chapman, then described to the committee his visit to the Lakeside Company headquarters. He had found many elements of the company's accounting system to be more appropriate to a smaller business but still judged the financial records to be auditable.

After reviewing all of the pertinent information, the review committee unanimously recommended that the firm actively pursue this engagement. Consequently, Abernethy met with Benjamin Rogers, president of Lakeside, during the subsequent week and an oral agreement was reached. Rogers explained that the Lakeside Board of Directors had to give final approval for changing auditors but their consent seemed assured. Several days later, Abernethy forwarded two copies of an engagement letter (see Exhibit 3-1) to Rogers who signed one copy and returned it to the CPA firm. Rogers also contacted the previous auditors, King and Company, and gave them formal permission to show the Lakeside working paper files to Abernethy and Chapman.

Three members of the organization were assigned to the engagement team: Dan Cline, partner; Wallace Andrews, manager; and Carole Mitchell, senior. In addition, several staff auditors were available to assist this group whenever necessary. There was also a consulting partner assigned. Although each of these auditors was involved in completing other engagements, a number of preliminary audit procedures were started during the months that followed. As the partner, Cline was responsible for the final review of all working papers produced during the Lakeside examination. To acquire the industry expertise needed to evaluate the client's financial reporting, he set out to learn as much as possible about the selling and distribution of audio equipment.

Meanwhile, Cline and the other members of the engagement team began to consider the various risks involved with this audit. As with all accounting firms performing audits, Abernethy and Chapman assume an amount of risk called acceptable audit risk. Acceptable audit risk (AAR) is a measure of how willing the auditor is to accept that the financial statements may be materially misstated even after the audit is completed and an unqualified opinion is given. If the firm accepts a low level of risk, then they have to be more certain that the financial statements are not materially misstated. For example, if the AAR is 10%, then the auditor has to be 90% confident that the financial statements are fairly stated, and if the AAR is 5%, then the auditor has to be 95% confident. Thus, there is an inverse relationship between the AAR and the firm's confidence in the fair presentation of the financial statements.

The next task of the engagement team is to determine the level of other risks associated with the audit--inherent risk, control risk and planned detection risk. To do this, they employed the audit risk model according to <u>Statement on Auditing Standards Number 47</u>. Under this model:

$$PDR = AAR/(IR \times CR)$$

where

PDR	=	planned detection risk
AAR	=	acceptable audit risk
IR	=	inherent risk
CR	=	control risk

Inherent risk is a measure of the firm's assessment of the likelihood that there are material misstatements before considering the effectiveness of the internal control structure. The evaluation of inherent risk is based upon the nature of the client's business and the susceptibility to misstatement in particular accounts. For example, due to the possibility of theft and the large number of transactions affecting the account, "cash" is normally considered to have a higher level of inherent risk than "prepaid expenses". Control risk is a measure of the firm's assessment of the likelihood that there are material misstatements that will not be prevented or detected by the client's internal control structure. The evaluation of control risk is based upon the effectiveness of Lakeside's internal control structure. For example, if the engagement team concludes that Lakeside's internal controls are poor, then control risk will be set at the maximum level. Planned detection risk is a measure of the firm's assessment of the likelihood that there are material misstatements that will not be detected by the firm's audit procedures, and is computed using the audit risk formula. For example, if AAR is 10%, IR is 100% (very high), and CR is 50% (moderate controls), then DR is computed using the audit risk model as:

PDR = AAR/(IR x CR)
    = .10/(1.0 x .50)
    = .20 or 20%

Andrews began to assess inherent risk by gaining an in-depth knowledge of Lakeside. He reviewed the working papers of the predecessor auditor and spent a number of days at Lakeside's headquarters studying various aspects of the business while also talking with key employees. In addition, he toured three of the retail stores and, at another time, questioned two of the regional sales representatives about the organization of the company's distributorship business.

Mitchell, the senior auditor, is in charge of assessing control risk. In the initial stages of the engagement, she and staff auditor Art Heyman are testing specific control policies and procedures. They are attempting to determine if control risk is below a maximum level. They have identified a number of controls at Lakeside and must now ensure that they are designed and operating efficiently.

Based on the assessments of inherent and control risks, Mitchell will determine the planned detection risk, which will allow her to recommend substantive auditing procedures for the Lakeside engagement. These substantive procedures will be capable (according to her judgment) of generating the sufficient, competent evidence needed to render a decision as to the fair presentation of the financial statements. However, before Mitchell's program is put into action, a review by both Cline and Andrews will be required. In most audits, the partner and manager are likely to feel that additional testing is needed in certain audit areas whereas less evidence may be adequate in others.

The partners of Abernethy and Chapman stress that risk levels must be constantly monitored throughout an engagement. Hence, before the final audit program is prepared, a thorough investigation is made to identify all critical audit areas within the client's financial records. A critical area is defined by the firm as any account balance, any procedure within a system, or any potential problem where either the materiality or the possibility of misstatement is so great as to threaten the fairness of the reported data. Although Mitchell understands that the determination of critical areas will influence the specific testing procedures to be included within the audit program, she also realizes that her firm has submitted a relatively low bid to get this engagement. Thus, she is aware that wasted time has to be avoided in order to complete the examination within the budgeted time period. By pinpointing any critical areas, Mitchell hopes to maximize audit efficiency.

One of the principal techniques used in identifying critical audit areas is an analytical review. According to <u>Statement on Auditing Standard Number 56 (Paragraph 6)</u>, the objective of analytical procedures "is to identify such things as the existence of unusual transactions and events, and amounts, ratios and trends that might indicate matters that have financial statement and audit planning ramifications." Analytical procedures do not necessarily indicate that a balance is correctly or incorrectly reported. However, if a recorded amount differs significantly from the expectation, additional investigation is warranted. There are five types of analytical procedures--those that compare the client's data with 1) industry data (such as industry average financial ratios), 2) similar prior period data (such as account balances in the previous year), 3) client-determined expected results (such as budgeted amounts), 4) expected results using nonfinancial information (such as square footage and shelf-space in a warehouse to estimate maximum inventory quantities) and 5) auditor-determined expected results (such as estimates from historical trends in accounts or financial ratios). Analytical review procedures are normally applied during the planning stages of an audit, as well as during the testing and final stages of an audit. Along with detailed testing of transactions and balances, analytical review procedures are considered substantive tests.

Mitchell visited the Lakeside headquarters on October 17, 1994 to begin performing analytical procedures on that company's financial information for the first nine months of the current year. Prior to this date, she had carefully reviewed the Lakeside financial statements for the past two years (Exhibits 3-2, 3-3, and 3-4). She also studied industry data developed for her by the audit partner, Dan Cline (Exhibit 3-5).

When Mitchell arrived at the client's headquarters, she obtained a trial balance from the controller's office (Exhibit 3-6). Before beginning her analysis, she discussed general ledger and trial balance procedures with Mark Hayes, the controller for Lakeside. He indicated that a trial balance is prepared every two weeks to provide company officials with current data. Copies of this trial balance are distributed to Mr. Rogers, Mr. Miller, Ms. Howell, Mr. Davis, and Mr. Thomas for their review (see Exhibit 4-1 for an organization chart). All ledger entries, except for inventory and cost of goods sold, come from a weekly posting of the company's journals. The various inventory figures are generated from a weekly summary sheet provided by the computer center that maintains Lakeside's perpetual inventory records. At the end of each quarter, estimated figures for depreciation and bonuses are included to present a more realistic net income figure for the period. Income taxes are also estimated by Hayes and paid quarterly to the government. In addition, to promote comparability in evaluating the stores, a monthly rental charge is included for Store 6. This figure, which is based on square footage and store location, is eliminated prior to preparation of external financial statements. However, company management believes that this expense is necessary for internal comparisons and decision-making.

DISCUSSION QUESTIONS

(1) Analyze the engagement letter prepared by Abernethy and Chapman (Exhibit 3-1). What specific responsibilities are being accepted by the CPA firm? What responsibilities are assigned to the client company?

(2) A client company will report balances for accounts such as Cost of Goods Sold. In order to perform analytical procedures, the auditor must develop expectations from as many sources as possible. The expected balance is then compared with the actual balance and any significant fluctuations are examined further. In the Lakeside case, what sources would be available to the auditor in arriving at an expected figure for Cost of Goods Sold?

(3) What critical audit areas would be inherent in a business such as the Lakeside Company? In other words, what accounts or transactions would have a high inherent risk?

(4) An audit program is designed to generate sufficient evidence on which the auditor can base an opinion. How does the auditor know when sufficient evidence has been accumulated?

(5) Mitchell is going to carry out analytical procedures on Lakeside's trial balance and other accounting data. What is the quality of the evidence that is gathered by this substantive testing procedure? That is, how competent is evidence provided by analytical review procedures compared with other types of evidence?

(6) The partner-in-charge of the audit, Dan Cline, is responsible for learning about the audio equipment business. How extensive should the auditor's knowledge of the industry be, and how does the auditor go about getting this type of information?

(7) Analytical procedures are performed again by the auditor in the final stages of an audit. What is the purpose of this final review?

(8) This case suggests that price competition with other CPA firms was an important factor in securing this audit engagement. What are the potential problems for a CPA firm that can arise from acquiring clients through price competition?

WRITTEN QUESTIONS

(1) Cline, Andrews and Mitchell agreed upon an acceptable audit risk (AAR) of 10% and an inherent risk (IR) of 80%. Using the audit risk model presented in the case and given the levels of AAR and IR determined by Cline, Andrews and Mitchell, write a report discussing the relationship between control risk and planned detection risk. Also, discuss the relationship between the level of planned detection risk and the relative amount of substantive tests (e.g., high, moderate, low) to be performed by the auditors. For example, if the PDR is high, does that mean the auditor should perform more or less substantive tests than otherwise? Using the audit risk model, give numerical examples to support your discussion.

(2) Prepare a worksheet indicating the analytical procedures that Mitchell should perform and show the results of these procedures. Among other things, consider comparing current results to prior years and current results to industry data. Also, consider computing financial ratios, such as the current ratio and the debt/equity ratio. Use the information presented in Exhibits 3-2 through 3-6. Create this worksheet using three columns. In the first, indicate the procedure that is being applied. In the second, note the results. In the final column, indicate the significance (if any) of the findings. An example of the worksheet format follows. (DISK: CASE3.WKS)

PROCEDURE	FINDINGS	SIGNIFICANCE
Scan the trial balance for unusual accounts or account balances	A debit balance appears in the Allowance for Doubtful Accounts	Bad accounts may be increasing or a debit entry may have been misposted.
Determine age of inventory (inventory/ [cost of goods sold/365]) and compare with prior years	Age as of 12/31/92 - 93.0 days. As of 12/31/93 - 100.5 days	Increase in age may indicate that company is holding obsolete or un-salable inventory, or that the year-end cut-off was incorrect

LIBRARY ASSIGNMENTS

(1) Read the following as well as any other published information concerning the risks encountered in an audit engagement:

"The Case for Risk-Driven Audits," Journal of Accountancy, March, 1989, p. 55.
"Audit Risk: How to Analyze It in Planning an Audit," The Practical Accountant, February, 1987, p. 51.
"Risks in the Foreground," Accountancy, March, 1989, p. 101.
"Audit Risk - Parts I and II," The CPA Journal, August, 1985, p. 12, and September, 1985, p. 34.
"Examination of the Effect of Risk Model Components on Perceived Audit Risk," Auditing: A Journal of Practice and Theory, Spring, 1991, p. 126.
"Audit Risk Assessment: A Discussion and Illustration of the Interrelated Nature of Statements on Auditing Standards," Woman CPA, Summer, 1990, p. 14.

The assessment of risk has become an important audit topic in recent years. Write a report identifying the types of risk that are found in an audit. Describe each of these risks. Discuss the methods by which the various risk levels are assessed by the auditor. Finally, describe the interrelationships among these risks.

(2) Read the following as well as any other published information concerning analytical review procedures:

"SASs Nos. 56 and 57: Increasing Audit Effectiveness," Journal of Accountancy, October, 1988, p. 56.
"An Analysis of Simple and Rigorous Decision Models as Analytical Procedures," Accounting Horizons, December, 1989, p. 79.
"Auditor Judgment in Analytical Review: Some Further Evidence," Auditing: A Journal of Practice and Theory, Spring, 1988, p. 22.
"A Study of Auditors' Analytical Review Performance," Auditing: A Journal of Practice and Theory, Spring, 1988, p. 1.
"Analytical Procedures: A Defensive Necessity," Auditing: A Journal of Practice and Theory, Spring, 1988, p. 150.

Write a report discussing the auditor's use of analytical review procedures in conducting an audit. What are the primary analytical procedures that auditors use? Why are analytical procedures necessary on an audit? How do they help an auditor be more efficient and effective? At what stages of an audit are analytical procedures applied?

Exhibit 3-1

Abernethy and Chapman
Certified Public Accountants
801 East Main Street
Richmond, Virginia 23235

July 17, 1994

Mr. Benjamin M. Rogers
The Lakeside Company
Box 887
Richmond, Virginia 23173

Dear Mr. Rogers:

    This letter will confirm our understanding concerning the examination of the financial statements of the Lakeside Company for the year ending December 31, 1994.

    Our examination will be performed in accordance with generally accepted auditing standards and, accordingly, will include such tests of the accounting records and such other auditing procedures as we consider necessary to enable us to express an opinion regarding these financial statements. This examination will be based on selective tests of recorded transactions. We will plan these tests and other procedures to search for material misstatements that may affect your financial statements. Within the inherent limitations of our test-based audit, we expect to obtain reasonable but not absolute assurance that major misstatements do not exist. If our investigation indicates the desirability of any changes in internal control procedures, we shall prepare a report on this subject for your consideration.

    Mr. Dan Cline will be the partner in charge of all audit work. He will inform you immediately if we encounter any circumstances which could significantly affect our fee estimate of $27,400 that was discussed with you this past week. Mr. Cline has suggested a due date of February 22, 1995 for the audit report. For our work to be as efficient as possible, we understand that your staff will provide a year-end trial balance by January 17, 1995 and an interim trial balance for the first three quarters of the year by October 17, 1994. In addition, your staff will provide us with certain working papers which we shall discuss with you in the next few days.

Exhibit 3-1 (Continued)

Page 2
Mr. Benjamin M. Rogers

    If these specifications are in accordance with your understanding of the terms of our engagement, please sign below and return the duplicate copy of this letter to us.

                      Yours truly,

                      Richard Abernethy, CPA
                      Abernethy and Chapman

Accepted by _____

Date _____

Exhibit 3-2
Lakeside Company
INCOME STATEMENT
For Year Ending December 31, 1994

	COMPANY STORES	DISTRIBU-TORSHIP	LAKESIDE TOTALS
Sales	$2,658,000	$3,120,000	$5,778,000
Sales Returns and Discounts	(168,000)	(233,000)	(401,000)
Net Sales	$2,490,000	$2,887,000	$5,377,000
Cost of Goods Sold	(1,608,000)	(1,827,000)	(3,435,000)
Gross Profit	$ 882,000	$1,060,000	$1,942,000
Salaries, Commissions, Bonuses	(641,000)	(380,000)	(1,021,000)
Advertising and Selling Expenses	(89,000)	(127,000)	(216,000)
Rent Expense	(121,000)	(25,000)	(146,000)
Depreciation Expense	(34,000)	(12,000)	(46,000)
Other General and Administrative Expenses	(102,000)	(93,000)	(195,000)
Interest Expense	(70,000)	(44,000)	(114,000)
Income Before Income Taxes	($ 175,000)	$ 379,000	$ 204,000
Income Taxes	70,000	(152,000)	(82,000)
Net Income	($ 105,000)	$ 227,000	$ 122,000
Retained Earnings, January 1, 1994			257,000
Cash Dividends			(67,000)
Retained Earnings, December 31, 1994			$ 312,000

Lakeside Company
INCOME STATEMENT
For Year Ending December 31, 1993

	COMPANY STORES	DISTRIBU-TORSHIP	LAKESIDE TOTALS
Sales	$2,526,000	$2,646,000	$5,172,000
Sales Returns and Discounts	(131,000)	(194,000)	(325,000)
Net Sales	$2,395,000	$2,452,000	$4,847,000
Cost of Goods Sold	(1,518,000)	(1,566,000)	(3,084,000)
Gross Profit	$ 877,000	$ 886,000	$1,763,000
Salaries and Commissions	(581,000)	(335,000)	(916,000)
Advertising and Selling Expenses	(91,000)	(112,000)	(203,000)
Rent Expense	(96,000)	(18,000)	(114,000)
Depreciation Expense	(33,000)	(12,000)	(45,000)
Other General and Administrative Expenses	(81,000)	(93,000)	(174,000)
Interest Expense	(52,000)	(35,000)	(87,000)
Income Before Income Taxes	($ 57,000)	$ 281,000	$ 224,000
Income Taxes	23,000	(112,000)	(89,000)
Net Income	($ 34,000)	$ 169,000	$ 135,000
Retained Earnings, January 1, 1993			193,000
Cash Dividends			(71,000)
Retained Earnings, December 31, 1993			$ 257,000

Exhibit 3-3

Lakeside Company
BALANCE SHEET

	DECEMBER 31, 1993		DECEMBER 31, 1994	
ASSETS				
Current Assets				
Cash		$ 68,000		$ 71,000
Accounts Receivable-Distributorship	293,000		388,000	
Allowance for Doubtful Accounts	(19,000)	274,000	(24,000)	364,000
Inventory - FIFO costing; lower of cost or market		786,000		946,000
Total Current Assets		$1,128,000		$1,381,000
Land, Buildings, and Equipment				
Land		$ 149,000		$ 149,000
Buildings and Equipment	337,000		348,000	
Accumulated Depreciation	(143,000)	194,000	(179,000)	169,000
Total Land, Buildings, and Equipment		$ 343,000		$ 318,000
Intangible Assets				
Leasehold Improvements	208,000		211,000	
Accumulated Depreciation	(86,000)	$ 122,000	(96,000)	$ 115,000
Total Assets		$1,593,000		$1,814,000

LIABILITIES AND STOCKHOLDERS' EQUITY

Current Liabilities				
Notes Payable - Current		$ 20,000		$ 20,000
Notes Payable - Trade		549,000		696,000
Accounts Payable - Cypress		156,000		166,000
Accrued Expenses and Taxes Payable		106,000		135,000
Total Current Liabilities		$ 831,000		$1,017,000
Notes Payable - Long-Term		355,000		335,000
Total Liabilities		$1,186,000		$1,352,000
Stockholders' Equity				
Common Stock - 10,000 shares issued and outstanding, $1.00 Par Value		$ 10,000		$ 10,000
Additional Paid-In Capital		140,000		140,000
Retained Earnings		257,000		312,000
Total Stockholders' Equity		$ 407,000		$ 462,000
Total Liabilities and Stockholders' Equity		$1,593,000		$1,814,000

Exhibit 3-4

Lakeside Company

STATEMENT OF CASH FLOWS

	Year Ending December 31, 1993		Year Ending December 31, 1994	
Cash Flows from Operating Activities:				
Received Cash from Customers	$4,811,000		$5,287,000	
Paid Cash for Goods to Be Sold	(3,016,000)		(3,438,000)	
Paid Cash for Selling Expenses	(203,000)		(216,000)	
Paid Cash for General and Administrative Expenses	(1,277,000)		(1,343,000)	
Paid Cash for Interest	(87,000)		(114,000)	
Paid Cash for Taxes	(86,000)	$142,000	(72,000)	$104,000
Cash Flows from Investing Activities:				
Acquired Additional Land, Building, and Equipment	$(32,000)		$(11,000)	
Acquired Additional Leasehold Improvements	(17,000)	(49,000)	(3,000)	(14,000)
Cash Flows From Financing Activities:				
Paid Current Note Payable	$(20,000)		$(20,000)	
Paid Cash Dividend	(71,000)	(91,000)	(67,000)	(87,000)
Net Increase in Cash		$ 2,000		$ 3,000
Schedule of Noncash Financing and Investing Activities:				
Note Payable Signed to Finance Construction of New Store		$154,000		$ -0-

Exhibit 3-5

National Federation of American Businesses

STUDY OF ANNUAL REPORTS

Fiscal Years Ending Between April 1, 1993 and March 31, 1994

	Audio Equipment Retail Stores	Audio Equipment Distributorships
Common Size Statements		
Sales	100%	100%
Sales Returns and Discounts	5%	9%
Cost of Goods Sold	58%	55%
Salary and Commission Expenses	16%	11%
Advertising and Selling Expenses	5%	6%
Rent Expense	4%	1%
Depreciation Expense	2%	2%
Other General and Administrative Expenses	3%	5%
Interest Expense	3%	1%
Net Income Before Income Taxes	4%	10%
Debt/Equity Ratio	2.0	1.4
Current Ratio	1.9	1.6
Inventory Turnover	3.9	4.6
Average Age - Trade Receivables (days)	34.2	46.9
Sales/Working Capital	9.5	10.8

Exhibit 3-6

Lakeside Company

TRIAL BALANCE - GENERAL LEDGER (Prepared by Client)

Account Numbers	Accounts	September 30, 1993 Debit	Credit	September 30, 1994 Debit	Credit
100-1	Cash - General	28,600		26,200	
100-2	Cash - Payroll	-		-	
100-3	Cash - Restricted	37,500		42,500	
101-1	Receivables - Distributorship	329,300		427,400	
101-2	Allowance for Doubtful Accts		8,400		4,300
102-1	Inventory - Warehouse	642,500		762,200	
103-1	Inventory - Store 1	33,300		38,800	
103-2	Inventory - Store 2	22,700		34,400	
103-3	Inventory - Store 3	39,800		60,400	
103-4	Inventory - Store 4	17,100		24,600	
103-5	Inventory - Store 5	34,900		34,100	
103-6	Inventory - Store 6	21,900		24,900	
110-1	Land	149,000		149,000	
111-1	Building - Warehouse/Office	163,500		163,500	
111-6	Building - Store 6	128,400		128,400	
112-1	Accumulated Depreciation - Warehouse/Office		113,000		125,600
112-6	Accumulated Depreciation - Store 6		29,600		35,400
115-1	Equipment	28,900		31,100	
116-1	Accumulated Depreciation - Equipment		12,200		16,600
120-1	Trucks and Vehicles	27,200		27,200	
121-1	Accumulated Depreciation - Trucks and Vehicles		18,100		22,500
125-1	Leasehold Improvements	211,000		211,000	
126-1	Accumulated Depreciation - Leasehold Improvements		94,000		105,000
200-1	Bank Credit Line - Federal First Bank		418,100		411,800

Exhibit 3-6 (Continued)

Account Numbers	Accounts	September 30, 1993 Debit	September 30, 1993 Credit	September 30, 1994 Debit	September 30, 1994 Credit
200-2	Bank Credit Line - Security National Bank		324,100		378,100
210-1	Accounts Payable - Cypress		161,600		206,700
220-1	Accrued Expenses Payable		-		-
220-2	Income Taxes Payable		-		-
220-3	Payroll Taxes Payable		4,100		6,200
220-4	Sales Taxes Payable		18,600		20,200
230-1	Estimated Bonus Liability		6,000		19,500
240-1	Notes Payable - Current		20,000		20,000
240-2	Notes Payable - Long-Term		340,000		390,000
300-1	Common Stock		10,000		10,000
310-1	Additional Paid-In Capital		140,000		140,000
400-1	Retained Earnings		257,000		312,000
410-1	Dividends	48,700		31,400	
500-1	Sales - Store 1		273,500		319,900
500-2	Sales - Store 2		397,800		398,900
500-3	Sales - Store 3		236,100		458,800
500-4	Sales - Store 4		242,300		265,400
500-5	Sales - Store 5		373,000		364,600
500-6	Sales - Store 6		110,800		121,200
510-1	Sales - District A		324,200		368,100
510-2	Sales - District B		414,800		444,000
510-3	Sales - District C		392,500		415,700
510-4	Sales - District D		330,800		404,800
510-5	Sales - District E		338,800		345,200
510-6	Sales - District F		424,400		469,900
520-1	Sales Returns - Stores	100,400		173,400	
520-2	Sales Returns - Distributorship	155,700		232,000	
525-1	Discounts - Distributorship	15,600		14,800	
550-1	Cost of Goods Sold - Store 1	162,600		185,300	

Exhibit 3-6 (Continued)

Account Numbers	Accounts	September 30, 1993 Debit	Credit	September 30, 1994 Debit	Credit
550-2	Cost of Goods Sold - Store 2	239,300		228,400	
550-3	Cost of Goods Sold - Store 3	138,200		231,000	
550-4	Cost of Goods Sold - Store 4	137,200		152,400	
550-5	Cost of Goods Sold - Store 5	229,000		218,000	
550-6	Cost of Goods Sold - Store 6	68,100		73,800	
555-1	Cost of Goods Sold - Distributorship	1,288,400		1,409,100	
580-1	Salary Expense - Store 1	45,200		51,200	
580-2	Salary Expense - Store 2	59,200		59,300	
580-3	Salary Expense - Store 3	39,300		40,400	
580-4	Salary Expense - Store 4	38,600		41,200	
580-5	Salary Expense - Store 5	54,800		55,100	
580-6	Salary Expense - Store 6	32,300		32,200	
585-1	Estimated Bonus Expense	6,000		19,500	
590-1	Sales Commissions - District A	18,600		20,900	
590-2	Sales Commissions - District B	23,900		25,400	
590-3	Sales Commissions - District C	22,600		23,600	
590-4	Sales Commissions - District D	19,000		27,000	
590-5	Sales Commissions - District E	19,500		19,400	
590-6	Sales Commissions - District F	24,400		26,600	
595-1	Administrative and Warehouse Salaries	275,400		303,600	
598-1	Payroll Taxes Expense	40,700		44,900	
600-1	Advertising Expense - Stores	66,700		64,200	
600-2	Advertising Expense - Distributorship	9,100		7,500	
605-1	Travel Expenses - Salesmen	66,200		74,900	
610-1	Freight-Out	19,800		25,300	
615-1	Rent Expense - Stores	105,200		114,700	
615-2	Rent Expense - Vehicles	17,600		15,600	
615-3	Rent Expense - Equipment	6,100		4,700	

Exhibit 3-6 (Continued)

Account Numbers	Accounts	September 30, 1993 Debit	Credit	September 30, 1994 Debit	Credit
616-1	Intracompany Rent Charge-Store 6		12,000		12,000
620-1	Depreciation Expense	37,900		38,200	
625-1	Computer and Accounting Services	10,200		12,600	
630-1	Legal and Auditing Expenses	10,700		9,100	
640-1	Repairs and Maintenance	19,100		48,900	
645-1	Supplies Expense	5,100		4,300	
650-1	Utilities Expense	44,600		36,400	
660-1	Bad Debt Expense	-		-	
670-1	Property Tax Expense	13,100		21,100	
680-1	Other Miscellaneous Expenses	39,900		33,600	
690-1	Interest Expense	81,200		89,100	
695-1	Income Tax Expense	75,000		92,000	
800-1	Gain on Disposition of Fixed Asset		-		14,000
	TOTALS	5,845,800	5,845,800	6,622,100	6,622,100

CASE 4

INTERNAL CONTROL STRUCTURE--ASSESSING CONTROL RISK

The CPA firm of Abernethy and Chapman was hired in July of 1994 to audit the financial statements of the Lakeside Company for the year ending December 31, 1994. Even though the year-end was nearly six months away, the firm began its preparation almost immediately.

Wallace Andrews and Art Heyman, a staff accountant with Abernethy and Chapman, spent a number of days doing preliminary analysis at Lakeside's headquarters. During this time, they also visited King and Company to review the working papers created during previous audits. Heyman was assigned to study the permanent file to learn more about the various accounting systems and internal control features that were in place at the Lakeside Company. While examining these documents, Heyman discovered an organization chart that King and Company had drawn to represent the client's internal structure (see Exhibit 4-1). He also found the symbols used by the previous auditors in flowcharting the company's various systems (see Exhibit 4-2).

Heyman next came to a section of the permanent file entitled "Revenue and Cash Receipts Cycle - Distributorship." Apparently, this portion of the audit work was performed originally by two people. The "Revenue Recognition" function had been described in a memo (see Exhibit 4-3) whereas the "Cash Receipts" section of the company was captured in flowchart form (see Exhibit 4-4). Heyman analyzed both of these systems in detail to familiarize himself with the organization and operations of the Lakeside Company.

After finishing the initial investigation of Lakeside, Andrews and Heyman held a discussion with Dan Cline, the audit partner who had been placed in charge of the actual engagement. This group met to discuss their understanding of the client's internal control structure, a procedure necessary for audit planning purposes. They also wanted to make an initial assessment of control risk, the auditor's expectation that a material misstatement would not be prevented or detected on a timely basis by Lakeside's internal control structure.

The auditor's evaluation of control risk has a significant impact on the nature, timing, and extent of substantive auditing procedures. Thus, this assessment is made early in the examination. Maximum control risk will normally lead the auditors to test more extensively using more experienced personnel. Conversely, if control risk is judged to be below the maximum level, overall audit time and effort may possibly be reduced. However, to justify a lower assessment of risk, additional tests of the controls are necessary. After identifying specific client policies and procedures that could prevent material misstatements, the auditors have to verify both the design of these controls and their effectiveness.

To ensure an adequate understanding of the internal control structure as well as to help assess the possibility of less than maximum control risk, Cline posed several questions to Andrews and Heyman:

- Has Lakeside established the proper environment for strong internal control? Is the management aware of the importance of internal control? Does management work to ensure that the internal control structure is constantly functioning in an appropriate fashion?

- Are the accounting systems appropriately designed and monitored in order to allow for the proper creation and control of all financial records and other accounting information? Are the accounting systems able to identify all transactions and record them in a timely manner?

- Has the company established control policies and procedures such as the use of adequate documents? Do transactions have to be authorized? Are duties properly segregated to prevent irregularities?

- What other factors should be considered in reviewing Lakeside's internal control structure?

DISCUSSION QUESTIONS

(1) What kinds of information should Andrews have gathered during the preliminary stage of this audit in order to answer Cline's questions about the internal control structure? What sources are available to the auditors to help understand the client's internal control structure and assess its control risk?

(2) From the information provided to this point (including Exhibits 4-3 and 4-4), what answers can be given to Cline's questions? Mention the strengths as well as any weaknesses that have been found that will have a bearing on the auditor's assessment of control risk.

(3) After an initial assessment has been made of Lakeside's control risk, what possible actions can be taken by the auditors?

(4) As indicated, Mitchell is in the process of assessing control risk. What tests can an auditor perform to determine whether or not the control procedures are operating effectively?

WRITTEN QUESTIONS

(1) To gain an understanding of the client's present accounting systems, the firm of Abernethy and Chapman has a policy that all systems must be recorded in a memo (i.e., narrative) format and a flowcharting format. By using both, staff members are able to achieve a more effective and a more efficient understanding of the design of each system.

    a. Based on Exhibit 4-3 (a memo explanation of the Revenue Recognition section of the Revenue and Cash Receipts cycle), prepare a flowchart to provide a graphic display of this system. Use the flowchart symbols that appear in Exhibit 4-2.

    b. Analyze Exhibit 4-4, a flowchart representation of the Cash Receipts procedures, and prepare a written memorandum to accompany and explain this particular system.

(2) At the firm of Abernethy and Chapman, after the memo and flowchart have been prepared, a preliminary analysis is made of the internal control policies and procedures found in the system. The auditor is searching for weaknesses within the structure of the system as well as any particularly strong features that would reduce control risk. To assist the auditor in evaluating a system, Abernethy and Chapman utilizes the form presented in Exhibit 4-5. Complete this document based on the flowchart in Exhibit 4-4 representing the Cash Receipts section of the Revenue and Cash Receipts cycle. Be especially careful to note any internal control weaknesses or strengths that may be indicated. (DISK: CASE4.DOC)

(3) Rogers has stated that he wants the auditing firm to help improve Lakeside's accounting systems. Exhibit 4-3 identifies the revenue recognition procedures currently used in connection with distributorship sales. List improvements that could be made in this system.

LIBRARY ASSIGNMENT

(1) Read the following as well as any other published information concerning the audit consideration to be given to a client's internal control structure:

"Consideration of the Internal Control Structure in a Financial Statement Audit," Statement on Auditing Standards 55, issued by the Auditing Standards Board of the American Institute of Certified Public Accountants, April, 1988.

"SAS No. 55: The Auditor's New Responsibility for Internal Control," Journal of Accountancy, May, 1988, p. 86.

"Applying SAS No. 55 in Audits of Small Businesses," <u>Journal of Accountancy</u>, November, 1988, p. 40.

"A Critique of SAS No. 55," <u>Accounting Horizons</u>, March, 1991, p. 1.

Assume that an auditing firm has assessed the control risk of a new client to be below the maximum. Write a report describing the factors that could have led to this judgment. Indicate, also, the various effects that this evaluation could have on the audit testing process.

Exhibit 4-1

Lakeside Company

ORGANIZATION CHART

In Effect December 31, 1993

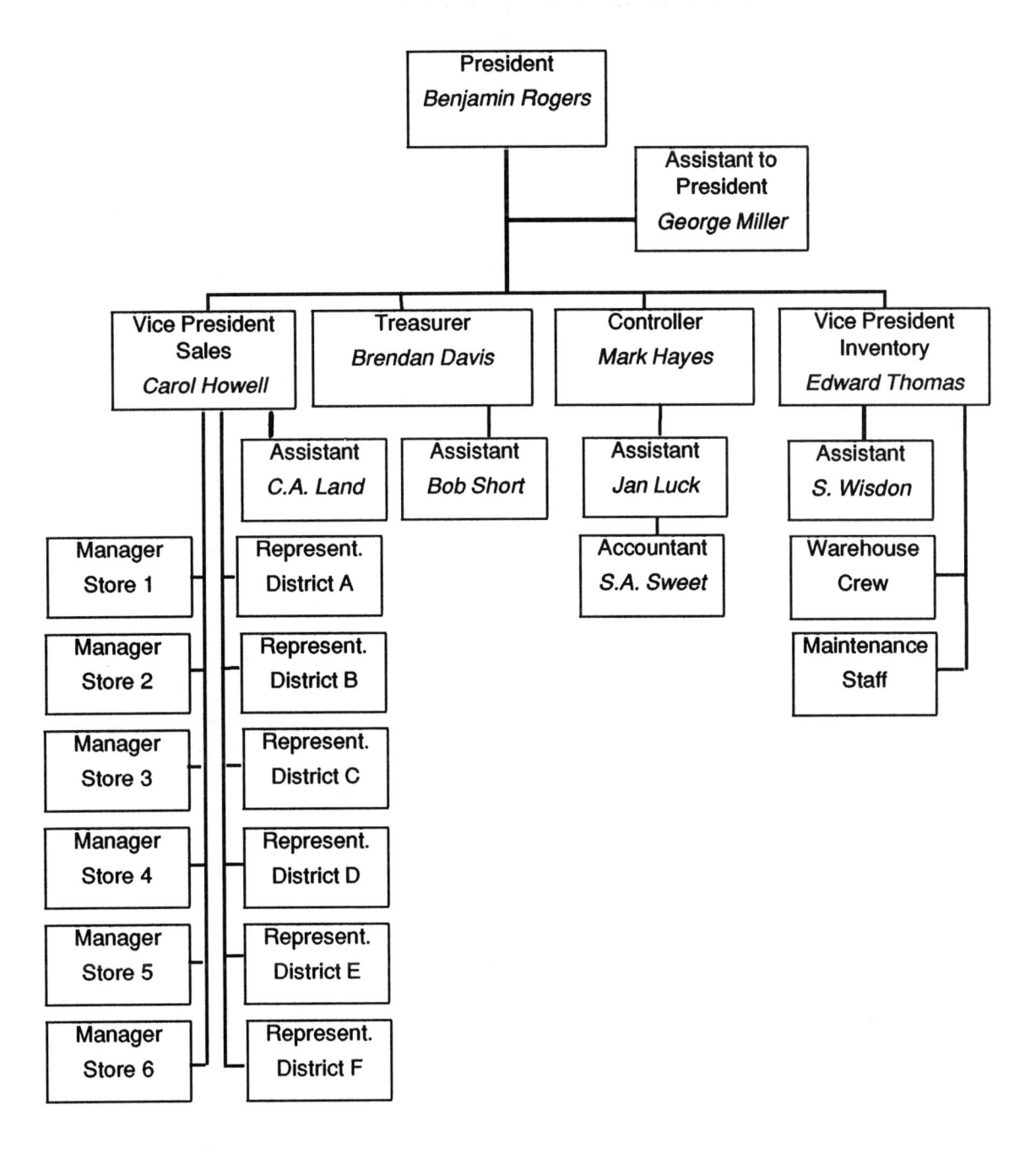

- **President** — *Benjamin Rogers*
  - **Assistant to President** — *George Miller*
  - **Vice President Sales** — *Carol Howell*
    - Manager Store 1
    - Manager Store 2
    - Manager Store 3
    - Manager Store 4
    - Manager Store 5
    - Manager Store 6
    - **Assistant** — *C.A. Land*
      - Represent. District A
      - Represent. District B
      - Represent. District C
      - Represent. District D
      - Represent. District E
      - Represent. District F
  - **Treasurer** — *Brendan Davis*
    - **Assistant** — *Bob Short*
  - **Controller** — *Mark Hayes*
    - **Assistant** — *Jan Luck*
      - **Accountant** — *S.A. Sweet*
  - **Vice President Inventory** — *Edward Thomas*
    - **Assistant** — *S. Wisdon*
      - Warehouse Crew
      - Maintenance Staff

Exhibit 4-2
King and Company
STANDARD FLOWCHART SYMBOLS

Terminal	Document	Manual Operation
Permanent File	Temporary File	Flow Lines
Annotation	Decision	Accounting Record
Calculator Tape	On-Page Connector	Off-Page Connector

Exhibit 4-3

CLIENT COMPANY: Lakeside Company

SYSTEM: Revenue and Cash Receipts Cycle - Distributorship

MEMO PREPARATION: Horace Clarke - 12/02/92

SYSTEM REVIEW AND UP-DATE:

Part A - Revenue Recognition - Distributorship

All distributorship sales are made by telephone. Either the customer or a Lakeside representative calls in each order. The Sales Division immediately records the incoming data on a prenumbered invoice which serves initially as a sales order form. This document is prepared in five copies with the last three being retained by the Sales Division in a temporary file by invoice number. The first copy is sent to Stan Wisdon in the Inventory Department who verifies the availability of the purchased items. If the merchandise is in the warehouse, it can be sent out almost immediately. However, if any items must be ordered from Cypress, the waiting time may be as long as three weeks. Wisdon estimates the ship-out date, completes and initials the sales invoice, and returns it to the Sales Division.

The second copy of the sales invoice goes to George Miller, Assistant to the President. Miller maintains the accounts receivable subsidiary ledger. He also keeps a list of approved customers with maximum credit limits. However, acceptance of new customers and changes in available credit are decisions made solely by Mr. Rogers, the president. Before approving any sale, Miller checks the current age of the customer's accounts receivable balance. If the store is on the approved list, is under the credit limitation, and has no overdue balances, Miller initials the sales invoice and returns it to the Sales Division. If, for any reason, Miller cannot approve the sale, the invoice is forwarded to Rogers who reviews all pertinent information. He then makes a final decision as to whether to accept or reject the order. Rogers indicates his decision on the invoice and forwards it to the Sales Division. If the order is rejected, the customer is contacted and all copies of the sales invoice are attached and placed in a permanent file by invoice number.

Exhibit 4-3 (Continued)

For approved orders, the Sales Division matches all five copies of the sales invoice. The approximate shipping date is indicated on the fifth copy and mailed to the customer as a confirmation. The first copy is initialled by C. A. Land in the Sales Division and returned to Wisdon in the Inventory Department as approval for making the shipment. The other three copies of the sales invoice are stamped "Approved" and remain in the Sales Division in a temporary file by invoice number.

Upon receiving the approved sales invoice, the Inventory Department packs and ships the merchandise and Wisdon prepares a five-copy bill of lading. One copy is included with the shipment while the second copy is mailed to the customer. The third copy is routed to the Controller's Office. The fourth copy of the bill of lading goes to the Sales Division with the final copy being retained by the Inventory Department. It is stapled to the first copy of the sales invoice and placed in a permanent file, by bill of lading number.

When the third copy of the bill of lading is received by Ms. Luck in the Controller's Office, the quantity of inventory, its description, the bill of lading number, and the date of shipment are recorded in an inventory sales journal. Having entered the appropriate information, Luck places the bill of lading in a temporary file by sales invoice number which has been manually recorded on the document. Lakeside uses the services of an outside computer center to maintain a perpetual inventory record. At the end of each week, Luck forwards information on all sales and purchases to the center which then processes the data and returns updated records to the company.

When the fourth copy of the bill of lading is received in the Sales Division, Land matches it with the three approved copies of the sales invoice. He compares the quantity and description of the order with the items that were shipped. If they agree, he prices each sale from an updated price list that is maintained by the Sales Division. The sales invoices are then extended, footed, and the due date is added. The fourth copy of the bill of lading is attached to the second copy of the sales invoice and filed in a temporary file by due date. The third copy of the approved sales invoice is sent to Miller, Assistant to the President, while the fourth copy goes to the Controller's Office. Miller uses his copy to update the accounts receivable subsidiary ledger and then files the sales invoice in a permanent file by customer name. The Controller's Office matches the sales invoice to the bill of lading, verifies the pricing against an updated price list, and mathematically checks the extensions and footings. The sales

Exhibit 4-3 (Continued)

invoice is then recorded in the Sales Journal as a debit to Accounts Receivable and a credit to Sales. Sales figures are also classified by geographic district so that commissions can be appropriately accrued. Lakeside representatives receive a percentage of every sale made within a specified territory. After recording the sale, the bill of lading is placed in a permanent file by customer name. The controller then mails the sales invoice to inform the customer of the amount payable, the due date, and the discount terms. According to the invoice, payment should be made by check (payable to "Lakeside Company"). The customer is also asked to return the bottom portion of the sales invoice which indicates the customer's name, the sales invoice number, the gross amount payable, the discount terms, and the due date.

CLIENT COMPANY: Lakeside Company

Exhibit 4-4

PF/12 Prepared 9/10/91 jcd
Reviewed 11/11/91 JVB
2nd Review 12/10/92 JVB
EMR 11/30/93

SYSTEM: Revenue and Cash Receipts Cycle - Distributorship Cash Receipts

Notes	Treasurer's Office	Assistant to President	Sales Division	Controller's Office

Notes

A. Stamp each check "For Deposit Only," prepare bank deposit slip in duplicate and four-part cash remittance list indicating customer name, amount paid, and invoice number.

B. Match the individual sales invoice slips with sales invoice and bill of lading. Calculate appropriate discount and record on each copy of cash remittance list.

C. Compare bank deposit slip total to cash remittance list total. Randomly reconcile individual items. Update accounts receivable subsidiary ledger.

D. Refoot cash receipts and sales discounts. Record journal entry in cash receipts journal.

E. Prepare monthly bank reconciliation. Spot check cash remittance list totals and dates against bank statement.

Exhibit 4-5
Abernethy and Chapman
Internal Control Structure - Preliminary Analysis

Client: _____
System: _____
Date: _____
Prepared By: _____

List each document found in this system, the number of copies, and whether it is prepared internally or externally.

Answer each of the following questions. For each "no" answer, comment on whether an internal control weakness is indicated.

Question	Yes	No	Comment
1. Is each document within this system pre-numbered?			
2. Is the authority for completing each document clearly delineated?			
3. Are all documents subsequently reviewed by an independent party within the company?			
4. Are appropriate procedures clearly spelled out for completing and reviewing each document?			
5. Is the record-keeping function independent of the custody function at all points throughout the system?			

Question	Yes	No	Comment
6. Are all mathematical computations independently verified?			
7. Does record-keeping begin at the origin of the transaction?			
8. Are all transactions authorized?			

9. In the space below, indicate any other specific internal control features that have been built into this system.

10. In the space below, indicate any other specific internal control weaknesses that appear to be present in this system.

CASE 5

TESTS OF CONTROLS

Carole Mitchell, a supervising audit senior with the CPA firm of Abernethy and Chapman, has been assigned to the Lakeside Company engagement. Her primary responsibility is evidence-gathering in connection with the examination of financial statements for the year ending December 31, 1994. One of the audit areas that concerns Mitchell is the accounts receivable balance generated by the distributorship side of the company. On December 31, 1993, this account made up 20% of the client's total assets, and analytical procedures applied to the September 30, 1994 trial balance revealed several ominous signs relating to the current receivables. The average age of the outstanding accounts had jumped from 43.8 days, at September 30, 1993, to 53.0 days, as of the present September 30. Since the company sells to its customers on terms of 2/10; n/45, this calculation indicated to Mitchell that the average balance was presently overdue. In addition, the company's write-off of accounts had increased dramatically. For the first 9 months of 1993, only $10,600 in receivables were judged to be bad, while $28,300 were considered uncollectible during the same period in 1994. Consequently, she viewed the inherent risk in this area to be quite high.

In the latter part of October, Mitchell discussed her findings to date with Dan Cline and Wallace Andrews, audit partner and audit manager for the engagement. At that meeting, Mitchell outlined the critical areas as she perceived them within the Lakeside examination. She indicated that one of these potential problems was the company's accounts receivable. Because of her concern, Mitchell spent considerable time reviewing with Cline and Andrews the revenue and cash receipts cycle. All three were aware that receivables provide special opportunities for theft as well as the reporting of fictitious sales.

Because of the high level of inherent risk for receivables, Cline suggested that further testing be done in hopes of reducing the control risk initially assessed in this area. Otherwise, a considerable amount of substantive testing would be required of the audit team. Consequently, Mitchell was assigned to perform extensive testing to determine if adequate control procedures and policies exist and are operating effectively. Once this test of controls is finished, a decision can be reached as to the amount of substantive testing that is necessary.

Cline also asked Mitchell to consider possible internal control improvements that could be recommended to Lakeside. Benjamin Rogers, the president of the company, had indicated that he wanted the systems to improve as the organization grew. Cline was well aware that relations with the client would be improved if the auditing firm could propose viable enhancements to the company's controls.

Finally, at this same meeting, the audit team decided that the existence of some the accounts receivable balances would be confirmed directly with the Lakeside customers. Andrews suggested that balances as of November 30, 1994 (instead of December 31, 1994) be confirmed unless severe internal control problems were encountered. The decision as to whether confirmations should be positive or negative, along with the specific number of accounts to be confirmed, was left to Mitchell's judgment, subject to the approval of Cline and Andrews.

Mitchell began her evaluation of the internal control structure by identifying the control procedures incorporated within Lakeside's revenue and cash receipts cycle (see Exhibits 4-3 and 4-4). These systems record both the increases and decreases made to accounts receivable. In her opinion, a number of the procedures appear to be well designed for a company the size of Lakeside, but several problems do exist. For example, no separate credit and collection departments are maintained. Also, the limited size of the company's staff reduces the number of opportunities that are available for dividing responsibilities.

Less than two weeks later, Mitchell started her tests of controls. She began by seeking information that would enable her to answer control questionnaires such as the one presented in Exhibit 5-1. Each questionnaire had been designed by the CPA firm with potential control problems in mind. Mitchell anticipated being able to complete each of these documents after a series of conferences with Lakeside employees.

On November 3, 1994, Mitchell visited the Lakeside headquarters to discuss control matters with several responsible officials. Her first conversation was with George Miller, Assistant to the President. (Refer to Exhibits 4-3 and 4-4.)

AUDITOR: Who has access to the accounts receivable subsidiary ledger?
MILLER: I do since I maintain the ledger, but in our company, all records are really open. I imagine that anyone who needed information could come in and look at them.
AUDITOR: How often do you age the accounts receivable?
MILLER: Only at the end of the year. However, I can easily review a specific account and determine its age at any time that I want.
AUDITOR: Is the subsidiary ledger ever tested by anyone else within the Lakeside organization?
MILLER: The independent auditors examine it at least once a year. No other testing would seem necessary.
AUDITOR: If a customer complains that an invoice is incorrect, who is responsible for investigating the matter?
MILLER: The Treasurer's office opens all mail. They have been directed to send

	any such complaints to me. I pull the sales invoices from my file and see what the trouble is.
I personally get in touch with the customers to settle the problem.
AUDITOR:	How do you verify credit approval?
MILLER:	The sales representatives file reports providing credit data gathered about potential clients. Rogers reviews this information and sets a maximum credit figure. If the account ever becomes overdue or if the customer exceeds this limit, further shipments are halted unless approval is made by Rogers.
AUDITOR:	How often does Rogers approve a sale to such customers?
MILLER:	I really do not know. The invoice goes directly from Rogers to the Sales Division.
AUDITOR:	How are the company's sales representatives paid?
MILLER:	On a percentage commission based on their total sales.
AUDITOR:	Is any subsequent review made of these credit reports?
MILLER:	No. If payment is made, the company is considered a good credit risk. Any customer that does not pay is a bad risk.
AUDITOR:	Sales have risen; has Lakeside's credit policy been eased recently?
MILLER:	Not really; the sales representatives are excellent. They have been building a good group of new customers.
AUDITOR:	The average age of accounts receivable has increased to over 53 days which means that the average account is currently overdue. Why is that?
MILLER:	The stores that sell Cypress products are stocking up prior to Christmas. Sales are a little slow for them right now, so their payments are sometimes delayed. Our collections will be just fine again right after the Christmas rush.
AUDITOR:	Why have so many receivables been written off this year?
MILLER:	I am not sure. We may have been holding on to some accounts in hopes of collecting. Of course, we are also selling more; we probably generate more bad debts.
AUDITOR:	How do you determine bad debt expense?
MILLER:	We estimate our uncollectible accounts at the end of each year based on .7% of net credit sales made by the distributorship.
AUDITOR:	How did Lakeside arrive at .7%?
MILLER:	I don't know. I think we have always used that figure.
AUDITOR:	How is the decision made as to which specific accounts will actually be written off as uncollectible?
MILLER:	After 60 days without payment, the Sales Division pulls its copy of the sales invoice and rebills the customer. Thirty days later a third bill is mailed and the Sales Division notifies me. I contact the sales representative who then puts pressure on the customer. Subsequently, the sales representative reports directly to me concerning possible payment. Based on this information, I make the decision as to whether

	the account is collectible. Unless an obvious problem exists, we don't even think about writing off balances until they are 5 or 6 months old.
AUDITOR:	Does the Sales Division send any invoices after the third one is mailed at 90 days?
MILLER:	No, any further billing is done by me.
AUDITOR:	Does Rogers or anyone else at Lakeside verify the specific receivables that are deemed uncollectible?
MILLER:	No, although Rogers has instructed me to remove companies from the credit list when their balance becomes 5 months old. Obviously, no further sales are made to these customers until payment is received.
AUDITOR:	Can inventory possibly be shipped to a customer without prior credit approval?
MILLER:	No. Either Rogers or I must initial the sales invoice and return it to the Sales Division. Without those initials, the Inventory Department is not allowed to process the order.
AUDITOR:	Does anyone verify that the invoices are correct as to prices, goods, extensions, etc.?
MILLER:	The Sales Division rechecks quantities and descriptions. I verify the prices and extensions when I receive my copy of the sales invoice. Unfortunately, by the time I get around to extending and pricing, the invoices are already out to the customers. On several occasions, we have had to rebill a customer when I discovered an error.
AUDITOR:	Could a sale be made and the invoice get lost or just not be prepared so that the customer never gets billed?
MILLER:	I certainly hope not. Approved sales invoices are filed in the Sales Division. If the bill of lading never shows up, that division will eventually check into the shipment. Subsequently, the Sales Division retains a copy of the completed sales invoice, I receive a copy, and the Controller gets a copy. If one of these copies were to get lost, the other two departments would follow up on the matter.
AUDITOR:	What verification is made of the cash discounts that are taken by customers?
MILLER:	We are very tough on that issue. Our Sales Department recalculates all discounts. They allow credit only if deserved. If a company owes us $1,000 and pays $980, then $20 is still due unless the terms of the discount have been met.
AUDITOR:	I would like to get an aged schedule of your accounts receivable as of November 30. Will that be possible?
MILLER:	It is certainly inconvenient, but I imagine we can get that done.

After talking with Miller, Carole Mitchell prepared a program to test transaction details as well as the effectiveness of the control procedures in the revenue and cash receipts cycle. The steps in this program are presented in Exhibit 5-2.

DISCUSSION QUESTIONS

(1) What is the quality of the oral evidence that Mitchell is gathering from Mr. Miller?

(2) The case states that accounts receivable offer opportunities for theft. Provide several examples as to how such theft might be perpetrated.

(3) Cline also mentions that increased accounts receivable might indicate fictitious sales. How and why would fictitious sales be recorded?

(4) What information did Miller provide (or fail to provide) that would be troubling to an auditor?

(5) Under what conditions might the auditors omit testing the effectiveness of control procedures?

(6) Under the audit risk model, planned detection risk (PDR) is equal to the acceptable audit risk (AAR) divided by the product of inherent risk (IR) and control risk (CR): PDR = AAR/(IR x CR). The case states that inherent risk of a material misstatement of the account receivable balance is high. If the firm cannot reduce its evaluation of control risk to below the maximum level, how is planned detection risk affected? That is, what is the impact on detection risk of both a high level of inherent risk and a high level of control risk?

(7) What is the difference between positive and negative accounts receivable confirmations? When should one be used over the other?

(8) In selecting receivables to confirm, some accounts are normally chosen at random while others are specifically selected. What attributes indicate that a specific account receivable should be confirmed?

(9) As one testing procedure used in establishing the existence of reported amounts, the auditor will take a figure found in the financial statements and trace its components back through the various accounting records to the source documents created at the time of the original transactions. This list of forms, records, and documents leading through the accounting system is often referred to as an "audit trail." To accumulate evidence about the Accounts Receivable total, assume that you have been assigned to substantiate a number of debit entries in Lakeside's ledger account. For example, you select a $2,800 debit entry made on July 11, 1994. What items make up the audit trail for this amount and what information could be gathered from each? Indicate the degree of reliance the auditor should place on the data derived from these individual sources. Refer to Exhibit 4-3.

WRITTEN QUESTIONS

(1) Exhibit 5-1 contains the questions that Mitchell is to answer concerning accounts receivable control procedures. Using this case, as well as Exhibits 4-3 and 4-4, complete this questionnaire.

(2) Exhibit 5-2 is a portion of the audit program that Mitchell designed to test the operating efficiency of controls in the revenue and cash receipts cycle. For each individual test, indicate the anticipated results if the control procedure is working properly. Also, list the potential problems if the control is not functioning as designed.

LIBRARY ASSIGNMENT

(1) Read the following:

"Requiem for a Fraud," Forbes, December 26, 1988, p. 78.

Write a report indicating the similarities that exist between Coated Sales, Inc. and the Lakeside Company. In addition, assume that Lakeside is participating in the same types of fraud carried on by Coated Sales. Discuss the signs that have appeared in the first five cases that should alert the auditors to this problem.

Exhibit 5-1
Abernethy and Chapman
Control Testing Questionnaire-Accounts Receivable

Questions	Comments on Current System	Significance	Suggestions
(1) Is the subsidiary ledger reconciled by an indendent party on a regular basis?			
(2) Are appropriate, established criteria in place for writing off doubtful accounts?			
(3) Are accounts to be written off properly reviewed and authorized by an independent party?			
(4) Is an appropriate follow-up made on accounts that are written off?			
(5) Does the company periodically re-evaluate the method in use for estimating bad accounts?			
(6) Are customers billed regularly by a party separate from the subsidiary ledger?			
(7) Is an independent verification made of complaints from customers concerning their bills?			
(8) Was the company's policy of granting credit changed over the past year?			
(9) Can a credit sale possibly be made without prior credit approval?			
(10) Are credit files complete and periodically reviewed?			
(11) Are invoices verified as to agreement with goods shipped and price of goods?			
(12) Are extensions and footings recalculated?			
(13) Are cash discounts recomputed and verified as to actual days?			
(14) Can a sale possibly be made and goods shipped without an invoice being recorded or mailed?			

Exhibit 5-2
Abernethy and Chapman
Testing of Transactions Details and Controls
Lakeside Company Audit Examination
Revenue and Cash Receipts Cycle

(1) From the invoice file in the Sales Division, pick five invoices at random.*

    (A) Compare the sales invoice with the sales invoice slip.
    (B) Compare the sales invoice with the bill of lading.
    (C) Trace the amount of the remittance to the cash remittance list filed in the Controller's Office.
    (D) Recompute the appropriate discount and compare the discount taken according to the cash remittance list.
    (E) Verify the pricing of the invoice against an approved pricing list.
    (F) Extend and foot each invoice.
    (G) Trace the amount of the remittance to the validated bank deposit slip filed in the office of the Assistant to the President.
    (H) Trace the amount of the remittance to the Accounts Receivable Subsidiary Ledger.
    (I) Verify that each has been initialled by an appropriate official to indicate credit approval.

(2) From the Accounts Receivable Subsidiary Ledger, select three accounts at random. For each of these accounts, choose one debit entry and one credit entry.

For each debit entry:
    (A) Trace the amount to the sales invoice filed in the Sales Division and compare the amounts.

For each credit entry:
    (A) Trace the amount to the cash remittance list filed in the Controller's Office.
    (B) Trace the amount to the validated bank deposit slip filed in the Treasurer's Office.

(3) Select 10 customers on the approved customer list and verify that a credit report is on file and properly completed.

(4) Select 2 cash remittance lists at random. Foot the list and compare the total to the posting in the Cash Receipt Journal.

*Note: Sample sizes in practice would normally be larger than indicated here. Sample sizes have been kept small so they will be more manageable.

CASE 6

TESTING THE INVENTORY PROCUREMENT SYSTEM

Art Heyman is employed as a staff auditor with the independent accounting firm of Abernethy and Chapman. For the first two weeks of December 1994, Heyman is assigned to the Lakeside Company examination. During this period, he is to perform a number of testing procedures designed by Carole Mitchell, in-charge auditor on the engagement. At the present time, Heyman is beginning to analyze the transactions that occur in the client's merchandise procurement system. Within this testing, he is especially interested in determining the extent to which employees comply with control procedures while carrying out various required activities. This evaluation will influence the nature, timing, and extent of substantive tests to be performed by the firm in this area.

Lakeside utilizes perpetual inventory records generated by an outside service organization: a computer company called DATA Processing Systems of Richmond, Virginia. Every Friday, the Controller's Division of Lakeside forwards details of the past week's purchases and sales to DATA. The information is processed by the center so that updated records can be returned to the Lakeside offices by the following Monday afternoon. One copy of the current inventory balances goes to Edward Thomas, who is responsible for acquiring merchandise, while a second list is conveyed to Benjamin Rogers, president of the company.

Thomas analyzes the perpetual records each week noting inventory items that appear to be at a low-level. Based on this review, he prepares a purchase requisition to replenish Lakeside's depleted stocks. Virtually all merchandise is acquired directly from Cypress Products. The completed requisition includes the quantity being ordered as well as a description of the needed items. This document is then forwarded to Rogers for final review. Whenever the president disagrees or questions any part of the purchase, he discusses his concern with Thomas. If they decide to make a change, the original requisition is voided and a new one completed. After approval, Rogers routes one copy of the purchase requisition to the Treasurer, a second goes to the Controller, and the final copy is returned to Thomas. The original document serves as a purchase order and is mailed to Cypress.

Periodically, Thomas must also special-order merchandise from Cypress. Customer requests are often received for inventory that is not held in stock in the Lakeside warehouse. When Thomas receives notice that specific goods are needed, a purchase requisition is immediately prepared and forwarded to Rogers for approval.

When shipments arrive at Lakeside, the members of the Inventory Department unload the merchandise and inspect each item for damage. A receiving report is prepared indicating the identity, quantity, and condition of the goods. One copy of this document goes to the Treasurer's Office while another is routed to the Controller's Division where the inventory purchases journal is updated. Later, when the vendor invoice arrives from Cypress, it is stamped by Lakeside so that document numbers and individual verifications can be marked directly on the form. This invoice is matched by the Treasurer's Office with the purchase requisition and the receiving report to verify agreement. The prices shown for the acquired items are compared to a master price list and each invoice is extended and footed to establish mathematical accuracy. If all information is proper, the three documents are stapled together and placed in a due date file. On this date, the forms are removed and a check is prepared for the appropriate amount after reducing the balance for any cash discount being offered. The Treasurer writes "PAID" across the invoice and indicates the check number.

Lakeside's management makes several broad assertions regarding the inventory procurement system, as well as other systems and accounts: existence or occurrence, completeness, rights and obligations, valuation or allocation, and presentation and disclosure. Thus, Lakeside's management asserts that the inventory exists, that it is complete, that it belongs to them, that it is properly valued, and that it is properly presented in the financial statements along with appropriate disclosures. In evaluating these assertions, Mitchell and Heyman are aware that a variety of potential problems could exist: payment might be made for goods that were never received; Lakeside could fail to pay for merchandise, thus, incurring an unrecorded liability; the company may simply be paying incorrect amounts; etc. Consequently, within the audit program, Mitchell has designed audit procedures to test for the possibility of such occurrences, and, in general, to test all of the assertions made by management.

Although Heyman will perform a number of audit tests in this area, one procedure specifies the following individual steps:

- Select a date at random. From that day forward, list the amount and date of the next 12 checks found in the cash disbursements journal that are written to Cypress Products.

- Trace each of these 12 checks to the corresponding purchase invoice filed in the Treasurer's Office. Match the check information with the invoice for appropriate payment and dates.

- On each invoice, verify the presence of a physical notation indicating that a price check, extension, and footing were made by company employees.

- Re-extend and foot each invoice.

- Reconcile the prices charged on these invoices with the Master Price List filed in the Controller's Office.

- Locate each cancelled check and match it with the corresponding invoice for appropriate amount, payee, and date.
- Examine the corresponding receiving report and purchase requisition for each of the 12 transactions. Reconcile these documents with the purchase invoice, comparing quantity and specific identification of the acquired inventory items.

- Verify that each document has been properly authorized.

Heyman has already performed the steps listed above. His work and findings are documented in the workpaper presented in Exhibit 6-1. After completing this initial audit step, Heyman's next assigned procedure is as follows:

- Choose a date at random and, from the receiving report file located in the Inventory Department, select the next 12 receiving reports.

- Review these documents for completeness and authorization.

- Verify that each acquired item was properly recorded in the inventory purchases journal.

- For each of these receiving reports, locate the corresponding vendor invoice and purchase requisition filed in the Treasurer's Office. Verify the agreement of these three documents as to quantity of goods and description of acquired merchandise.

- Verify that the requisitions have each been approved by the proper company officials.

- On the invoice, note the client's indication that prices have been checked, extended, and footed.

- Reconcile the prices on the invoice to the Master Price List found in the Controller's Division.

- Locate the cancelled check for each invoice, matching the dollar amounts and recomputing any appropriate discount.

Heyman selected 12 receiving reports (Exhibit 6-2) and found the corresponding purchase requisitions (Exhibit 6-3) and vendor invoices (Exhibit 6-4). Heyman next located the cancelled checks for these 12 receiving reports (Exhibit 6-5). In addition, a portion of the Master Price List distributed by Cypress has been included in the CPA firm's working papers (Exhibit 6-6) along with a sample page reproduced from the client's inventory purchases journal (Exhibit 6-7).

DISCUSSION QUESTIONS

(1) What control procedures are evident in Lakeside's inventory procurement system?

(2) In the first set of testing procedures listed in this case, the auditor begins with cancelled checks and then seeks supporting documentation. In the second, receiving reports are selected and the recording of subsequent events is traced through the system. Which of the management assertions are being corroborated by each test? Why are the tests performed in these manners?

(3) The case mentions some possible purchasing and payment problems. Given the company's controls, is it possible that Lakeside might pay for goods not received? Is it possible that the company might fail to pay for inventory that has been received?

(4) What is the purpose of a workpaper such as the example presented in Exhibit 6-1? Does the workpaper belong to Lakeside or Abernethy and Chapman? Why?

(5) The first generally accepted auditing standard of field work states that assistants, if any, are to be properly supervised. Why is this requirement necessary and what supervision is indicated on the workpaper produced in Exhibit 6-1?

(6) What does the term "N-2" signify at the top of the workpaper presented in Exhibit 6-1? Explain this numbering system.

(7) On the workpaper, Heyman has included the objective, conclusions, and scope of this testing. Why is this information important on the workpaper?

(8) In Exhibit 6-1, on the right side of the workpaper, Heyman has indicated that three exceptions were found. Are these exceptions clearly explained by the auditor along with the ultimate resolution of each problem?

(9) At the bottom left side of the workpaper in Exhibit 6-1, Heyman has included, through the use of tick marks, a listing of audit procedures that were performed. Has he properly completed the steps listed in the audit program designed by Mitchell?

(10) Evaluate the workpaper in Exhibit 6-1 as to clarity and completeness.

WRITTEN QUESTION

(1) Details of the second part of Mitchell's audit program were described in the case narrative. Exhibits 6-2 through 6-7 provide the client records necessary to carry out these audit procedures. Perform the tests that were outlined and prepare a workpaper, similar to Exhibit 6-1, to present the work and the resulting evidence. If any problems are uncovered in carrying out these procedures, simply document them on the workpaper.

LIBRARY ASSIGNMENT

(1) Read the following as well as any other published information concerning financial statement assertions:

"Evidential Matter," Statement of Auditing Standards No. 31, issued by the Auditing Standards Board of the American Institute of Certified Public Accountants, August, 1980. (A copy of this pronouncement can be found in the November, 1980, Journal of Accountancy, pages 138-140.)
"Evidential Matter," The CPA Journal, January 1981, p. 70.

The Bethlehem Steel Company reported on its December 31, 1992 balance sheet a balance for inventory of $344.4 million. Write a short report describing and explaining the various assertions that the management of this company is making about this particular figure.

LAKESIDE COMPANY
INVENTORY PURCHASES AND CASH DISBURSEMENTS TRANSACTIONS EXHIBIT 6-1
12/31/91

W/P: N-2
AH 12/1/94
WJL 12/18/94
CM 12-6-91 DC 12/22/94

DATE	PAYEE	CHECK NUMBER	DOLLAR AMOUNT	AUDIT PROCEDURES	COMMENTS
1/4/91	CYPRESS PRODUCTS	961	12,610.47	✓ ∅ ✗ ✓ ∧ t n Ⓒ	Ⓐ Prices on purchases of 4/1/91 and 7/25/91 do not agree with master Price list by $200 and $360 respectively. According to Edmund Thomas, the difference represents monthly purchases from Cypress at different prices rather than shown on the current price list. C.M — was DC **PASS FURTHER WORK**
2/3/91		1480	391.05	✓ ∅ ✗ ✓ ∧ t n	
3/1/91		2322	4,210.46	✓ ∅ Ⓐ ✓ ∧ t n	
4/18/91		2568	6,069.10	✓ ∅ ✓ ✓ ∧ t n Ⓑ	
5/2/91		3113	841.70	✓ ∅ ✓ ✓ ∧ t n Ⓒ	
6/18/91		3694	7,018.45	✓ ∅ ✓ ✓ ∧ t n	Ⓑ Purchase requisition does not agree with receiving report for one item. Thomas indicated that replacement with a similar item was made because of stock-out. C.M — was DC **PASS FURTHER WORK**
7/25/91		4230	2,292.44	✓ ∅ Ⓐ ✓ ∧ t n	
8/4/91		4493	667.45	✓ ∅ ✓ ✓ ∧ t n	
9/13/91		5020	318.91	✓ ∅ ✓ ✓ ∧ t n	
10/20/91		5551	15,446.91	✓ ∅ ✓ ✓ ∧ t n	Ⓒ Four requisitions were approved by Miller rather than Rogers. Thomas indicated that only requisitions estimated to be over $1,000 must be approved by Rogers. C.M — was DC **CHANGE SYSTEM FLOWCHART PASS FURTHER WORK**
11/15/91		6009	861.70	✓ ∅ ✓ ✓ ∧ t n	
12/23/91		6681	2,098.78	✓ ∅ ✓ ✓ ∧ t n	

Audit Procedures:
- ✓ Traced to purchase invoice. Noted agreement with amount of check and posting date. Each disbursement is 3% less than the invoice amount, representing the cash discount. All discounts were recalculated.
- ∅ Compared invoice prices with master price list. All agreed except Ⓐ
- ✗ Examined purchase invoices for evidence that company employee initialed prices, extensions, and footings. Markings all initialed present in all cases.
- W Verified mathematical accuracy of extensions and footings of invoices.
- ∧ Examined cancelled check that amount, date, signature, endorsement & payee.
- t Examined receiving report for agreement with purchase invoice as to description and quantity. All agreed.
- n Examined purchase requisition. Goods properly signed by either Thomas or Wisdom. Invoice verified account code. All requisitions were properly approved except Ⓑ and Ⓒ.

Audit Objectives:
- To verify that all merchandise was properly ordered and received and is for legitimate business purposes.
- To verify that expenses and credits are properly valued and classified. To verify that seller disbursements are for legitimate commitments and properly recorded.

Audit Conclusion:
Purchase and disbursement transactions are fairly stated per the scope.

Scope:
(a) Population — All purchases from Cypress Products. Appear from Cash Disbursements journal.
(b) Sample — Judgmental. Selected 1/12 disbursements for merchandise from Cypress Products.

Exhibit 6-2

Lakeside Company Receiving Reports

No. 3918	Date 8/20/94	Inspected by Jones
Quantity	Description	Condition
20	Radios IB 23-D	good
5	Cassette decks HG 87-X	good

No. 3919	Date 8/21/94	Inspected by Jones
Quantity	Description	Condition
1	Amplifiers XX 99-T	good

No. 3920	Date 8/24/94	Inspected by Simon
Quantity	Description	Condition
1	Audio Component System BM 09-H	good
3	Receivers LM 12-T	good
2	Receivers FD 23-Y	good

No. 3921	Date 8/27/94	Inspected by Jones
Quantity	Description	Condition
4	Speakers YG 28-Y	good
2	Stereo Systems RT 45-I	good
2	Stereo Systems FU 87-R	good
10	Head Phones KJ 32-K	good
5	Radios BV 24-R	good
8	Turntables XW 55-P	good

Exhibit 6-2 (continued)

No. 3922	Date 8/28/94	Inspected by Nance
Quantity	Description	Condition
1	Audio Component System BD17-H	good
12	Amplifiers KI 34-Z	good

No. 3923	Date 9/2/94	Inspected by Jones
Quantity	Description	Condition
6	Turntables NB 67-C	good
6	Turntables XW 55-P	good
10	Turntables RW 21-X	good

No. 3924	Date 9/3/94	Inspected by Simon
Quantity	Description	Condition
30	Radios BV 24-R	good
20	Radios RA 01-O	good
2	Speakers BF 23-G	good

No. 3925	Date 9/7/94	Inspected by Nance
Quantity	Description	Condition
1	Stereo System RA 69-M	good

Exhibit 6-2 (continued)

No.	Date	Inspected by
Quantity	Description	Condition
	Receiving report #3926 was **not** on file!	

No. 3927	Date 9/14/94	Inspected by Nance
Quantity	Description	Condition
5	Amplifiers BC 76-W	good
4	Audio component systems BD 17-H	good
6	Receivers NB 73-X	good
2	Speakers BF 23-G	good
2	Stereo Systems XZ 23-U	good

No. 3928	Date 9/16/94	Inspected by Jones
Quantity	Description	Condition
1	Audio Component System AR 65-C	good
20	Head Phones PO 88-Q	good

No. 3929	Date 9	Inspected by Jones
Quantity	Description	Condition
60	Radios CB 21-S	good
10	Receivers NB 73-X	good

Exhibit 6-3

Lakeside Company Purchase Requisitions

Request: Thomas Date: 8/9/94			Request: Wisdon Date: 8/11/94	
No. **6702** Approval: Rogers Date: 8/10/94			No. **6703** Approval: Miller Date: 8/11/94	

Quantity	Description
20	Radios IB23-D
5	Cassette Decks HG87-X

Quantity	Description
1	Amplifier XX99-T

(For Office Use Only)
Receiving Report No. __3918__
Agreement With Order: OK Luck
Purchase Invoice Dated: 8/18/94
Agreement With Invoice: ✓ BS

(For Office Use Only)
Receiving Report No. __3919__
Agreement With Order: OK Luck
Purchase Invoice Dated: 8/19/94
Agreement With Invoice: ✓ BS

Exhibit 6-3 (continued)

Request: Thomas	Date: 8/17/94	
No. <u>6704</u> Approval: Rogers	Date: 8/19/94	

Quantity	Description
4	Speakers YG28-Y
2	Stereo Systems RT45-I
8	Turntables XW55-P
20	Headphones KJ32-K
5	Radios BV24-R
2	Stereo Systems FU87-R

(For Office Use Only)
Receiving Report No. <u>3921</u>
Agreement With Order: Only 10 headphones received. Rest back order. OK Luck
Purchase Invoice Dated: <u>8/23/94</u>
Agreement With Invoice: <u>✓ BS (except partial)</u>

Request: Wisdom	Date: 8/18/94	
No. <u>6705</u> Approval: Rogers	Date: 8/18/94	

Quantity	Description
1	Audio Component System BM09-H
3	Receivers LM12-T
2	Receivers FD23-Y

(For Office Use Only)
Receiving Report No. <u>3920</u>
Agreement With Order: OK Luck
Purchase Invoice Dated: <u>8/22/94</u>
Agreement With Invoice: <u>✓ BS</u>

Exhibit 6-3 (continued)

Request: Thomas Date: 8/18/94		
No. 6706 Approval: Rogers Date: 8/19/94		

Quantity	Description
12	Amplifiers KI34-Z
1	Audio Component System BD17-H

(For Office Use Only)
Receiving Report No. 3922
Agreement With Order: OK Luck
Purchase Invoice Dated: 8/26/94
Agreement With Invoice: ✓ BS

Request: Thomas Date: 8/24/94
No. 6707 Approval: Rogers Date: 8/25/94

Quantity	Description
6	Turntables NB67-C
6	Turntables XW55-P
10	Turntables CD00-N

(For Office Use Only)
Receiving Report No. 3923 Cypress re-
Agreement With Order: placed CD00-N with RW21-X. Thomas accepts
Purchase Invoice Dated: 8/31/94 OK Luck
Agreement With Invoice: ✓ BS (except 1)

Exhibit 6-3 (continued)

No. **6708**	Request: _Thomas_ Date: _8/26/94_ Approval: _Rogers_ Date: _8/26/94_
Quantity	**Description**
2	Speakers BF23-G
30	Radios BV24-R
20	Radios RA01-0

(For Office Use Only)
Receiving Report No. _3924_
Agreement With Order: _ok Luck_
Purchase Invoice Dated: _8/31/94_
Agreement With Invoice: _✓ BS_

No. **6709**	Request: _Thomas_ Date: _8/26/94_ Approval: _Rogers_ Date: _8/28/94_
Quantity	**Description**
10	Speakers KM98-G
6	Speakers VD34-L

(For Office Use Only)
Receiving Report No. _3926_
Agreement With Order: _ok Luck_
Purchase Invoice Dated: _9/4/94_
Agreement With Invoice: _✓ BS_

Exhibit 6-3 (continued)

Request: Thomas		Date: 8/28/94
No. 6710 Approval: Miller		Date: 8/28/94

Quantity	Description
1	Stereo System RA69-M

(For Office Use Only)
Receiving Report No. 3925
Agreement With Order: OK *Luck*
Purchase Invoice Dated: 9/3/94
Agreement With Invoice: ✓ BS

Request: Thomas		Date: 9/7/94
No. 6711 Approval: Rogers		Date: 9/8/94

Quantity	Description
4	Audio Component Systems BD17-H
5	Amplifiers BC76-W
2	Speakers BF23-G
2	Stereo Systems VC09-I
6	Receivers NB73-X

(For Office Use Only)
Receiving Report No. 3927
Agreement With Order: OK *Luck*
Purchase Invoice Dated: 9/11/94
Agreement With Invoice: ✓ BS

Exhibit 6-3 (continued)

	Request: Thomas Date: 9/8/94			Request: Thomas Date: 9/11/94
No. <u>6712</u>	Approval: Miller Date: 9/8/94		No. <u>6713</u>	Approval: Rogers Date: 9/14/94

Quantity	Description
1	Audio Component System AR65-C
20	Headphones PO88-Q

Quantity	Description
10	Receivers NB73-X
70	Radios CB21-S

(For Office Use Only)
Receiving Report No. 3928
Agreement With Order: OK Luck
Purchase Invoice Dated: 9/12/94
Agreement With Invoice: ✓ BS

(For Office Use Only)
Receiving Report No. 3929 CB21-S is 10 short and has been backordered.
Agreement With Order: Rest OK Luck
Purchase Invoice Dated: 9/18/94
Agreement With Invoice: ✓ BS (except above)

Exhibit 6-4

Vendor Invoices

Invoice 711				Invoice 802			
Cypress Products				Cypress Products			
Box 366 Silver Spring, MD				Box 366 Silver Spring, MD			
Shipped To: Lakeside Company, Box 887, Richmond, VA 23173		Date: 8/18/94 Terms: 3/20; N/60		Shipped To: Lakeside Company, Box 887, Richmond, VA 23173		Date: 8/19/94 Terms: 3/20 N/60	

Description	Qty.	Price	Total	Description	Qty.	Price	Total
Cassette Decks HG 87-X	5	74.75	373.75	Amplifier XX99-T	1	540.00	540.00
Radios IB 23-D	20	88.20	1764.00				

Paid Ck. # 3091

Paid Ck. # 3121

Lakeside Company
Date Received: 8/25/94
Rec. Rep. # 3918
Pur. Req. # 6702
Priced: BS
Footed: BS
Extended: BS

Lakeside Company
Date Received: 8/25/94
Rec. Rep. # 3919
Pur. Req. # 6703
Priced: BS
Footed: BS
Extended: BS

Total Amount Due	$2137.75	Total Amount Due	$540.00

Exhibit 6-4 (continued)

Invoice 991

Cypress Products
Box 366   Silver Spring, MD

Shipped To: Lakeside Company
Box 887
Richmond, VA 23173

Date: 8/22/94
Terms: 3/20 N/60

Description	Qty.	Price	Total
Audio Component System BM09-H	1	812.35	812.35
Receivers FD23-Y	2	146.99	293.98
LM12-T	3	234.65	703.95

Paid Ck #3164

Lakeside Company
Date Received: 8/27/94
Rec. Rep. # 3920
Pur. Req. # 6705
Priced: BS
Footed: BS
Extended: BS

Total Amount Due $1,810.28

Invoice 1261

Cypress Products
Box 366   Silver Spring, MD

Shipped To: Lakeside Company
Box 887
Richmond, VA 23173

Date: 8/23/94
Terms: 3/20 N/60

Description	Qty.	Price	Total
Turntables XW55-P	8	109.98	879.84
Speakers YG28-Y	4	274.95	1099.80
Stereo System RT45-1	2	165.98	331.96
Stereo Systems FU87-R	2	225.60	451.20
Radios BV24-R	5	32.30	161.50
Head Phones KJ32-K	10	24.95	249.50

Lakeside Company
Date Received: 8/29/94
Rec. Rep. # 3921
Pur. Req. # 6704
Priced: BS
Footed: BS
Extended: BS

Paid Ck #3203

Total Amount Due $3,173.80

Exhibit 6-4 (continued)

Invoice 1313				Invoice 1406			
Cypress Products Box 366 Silver Spring, MD				Cypress Products Box 366 Silver Spring, MD			
Shipped To: Lakeside Company Box 887 Richmond, VA 23173		Date: 8/26/94 Terms: 3/20 N/60		Shipped To: Lakeside Company Box 887 Richmond, VA 23173		Date: 8/31/94 Terms: 3/20 N/60	
Description	Qty.	Price	Total	Description	Qty.	Price	Total
Audio Component System BD17-H	1	1261.98	1261.98	Turntables NB67-C	6	85.32	511.92
Amplifiers KI34-Z	12	412.88	4954.56	Turntables XW55-P	6	109.98	659.88
				Turntables CD00-N	10	148.50	1485.00

Invoice 1313: *Paid Ck. # 3251*

Lakeside Company
Date Received: 9/1/94
Rec. Rep. # 3922
Pur. Req. # 6706
Priced: BS
Footed: BS
Extended: BS

Total Amount Due $6,216.54

Invoice 1406: *Paid Ck. # 3310*

Lakeside Company
Date Received: 9/5/94
Rec. Rep. # 3923
Pur. Req. # 6707
Priced:
Footed:
Extended:

Total Amount Due $2,656.80

Exhibit 6-4 (continued)

Invoice 1510				Invoice 1616			
Cypress Products Box 366 Silver Spring, MD				Cypress Products Box 366 Silver Spring, MD			
Shipped To: Lakeside Company Box 887 Richmond, VA 23173		Date: 8/31/94 Terms: 3/20 N/60		Shipped To: Lakeside Company Box 887 Richmond, VA 23173		Date: 9/3/94 Terms: 3/20 N/60	
Description	Qty.	Price	Total	Description	Qty.	Price	Total
Radios BV24-R	30	25.98	779.40	StereoSystem RA69-M	1	365.00	365.00
Radios RA01-O	20	87.95	1759.00				
Speakers BF23-G	2	469.00	938.00				

Invoice 1510: Paid Ck. # 3345

Lakeside Company
Date Received: 9/6/94
Rec. Rep. # 3924
Pur. Req. # 6709
Priced: BS
Footed: BS
Extended: BS

Total Amount Due $3,476.40

Invoice 1616: Paid Ck. # 3397

Lakeside Company
Date Received: 9/4/94
Rec. Rep. # 3925
Pur. Req. # 6710
Priced: BS
Footed: BS
Extended: BS

Total Amount Due $365.00

Exhibit 6-4 (continued)

Invoice 1691				Invoice 1812			
Cypress Products Box 366 Silver Spring, MD				Cypress Products Box 366 Silver Spring, MD			
Shipped To: Lakeside Company Box 887 Richmond, VA 23173		Date: 9/4/94 Terms: 3/20 N/60		Shipped To: Lakeside Company Box 887 Richmond, VA 23173		Date: 9/11/94 Terms: 3/20 N/60	
Description	Qty.	Price	Total	Description	Qty.	Price	Total
Speakers KM98-G	10	81.40	814.00	Amplifiers BC76-W	5	688.32	3441.60
Speakers VD34-L	6	123.40	740.40	Audio Component System BD17-H	4	1261.98	5047.92
				Receivers NB73-X	6	445.70	2674.20
Paid Ck #3425				Speakers BF23-G	2	469.00	938.00
				Stereo Systems VC09-1	2	210.34	420.68
Lakeside Company Date Received: 9/10/94 Rec. Rep. # 3926 Pur. Req. # 6709 Priced: BS Footed: BS Extended: BS				Lakeside Company Date Received: 9/17/94 Rec. Rep. # 3927 Pur. Req. # 6711 Priced: BS Footed: BS Extended: BS		Paid Ck.#3451	
Total Amount Due			$1,554.40	Total Amount Due			$12,522.40

Exhibit 6-4 (continued)

Invoice 2072				Invoice 2149			
Cypress Products Box 366 Silver Spring, MD				Cypress Products Box 366 Silver Spring, MD			
Shipped To: Lakeside Company Box 887 Richmond, VA 23173		Date: 9/12/94 Terms: 3/20 N/60		Shipped To: Lakeside Company Box 887 Richmond, VA 23173		Date: 9/18/94 Terms: 3/20 N/60	
Description	Qty.	Price	Total	Description	Qty.	Price	Total
Audio Component System AR65-C	1	1319.00	1319.00	Receivers NB73-X	10	445.70	4457.00
Head Phones PO88-Q	20	79.95	1599.00	Radios CB21-S	60	181.18	10,870.80

Invoice 2072: *Paid Ck # 3471*

Lakeside Company
Date Received: 9/18/94
Rec. Rep. # 3428
Pur. Req. # 6712
Priced: BS
Footed: BS
Extended: BS

Total Amount Due $2,918.00

Invoice 2149: *Paid Ck # 3510*

Lakeside Company
Date Received: 9/26/94
Rec. Rep. # 3429
Pur. Req. # 6713
Priced: BS
Footed: BS
Extended: BS

Total Amount Due $15,327.80

Exhibit 6-5

Lakeside Company

Checks

Lakeside Company 3091 Box 887 Richmond, VA 23173 Sept. 16, 1994 Pay Cypress Products $2,073.63 Two thousand seventy-three and 63/100 Dollars INV. #711 Brendan Davis	**Lakeside Company** 3121 Box 887 Richmond, VA 23173 Sept. 16, 1994 Pay Cypress Products $523.80 Five hundred twenty-three and 80/100 Dollars INV. #802 Brendan Davis
Lakeside Company 3164 Box 887 Richmond, VA 23173 Sept. 20, 1994 Pay Cypress Products $1,755.97 Seventeen hundred fifty-five and 47/100 Dollars INV. #991 Brendan Davis	**Lakeside Company** 3203 Box 887 Richmond, VA 23173 Sept. 20, 1994 Pay Cypress Products $3,046.85 Three thousand forty-six and 85/100 Dollars INV. #1261 Brendan Davis
Lakeside Company 3251 Box 887 Richmond, VA 23173 Sept. 21, 1994 Pay Cypress Products $6,030.04 Six thousand thirty and 04/100 Dollars INV. #1313 Brendan Davis	**Lakeside Company** 3310 Box 887 Richmond, VA 23173 Sept. 28, 1994 Pay Cypress Products $2,577.10 Twenty-five hundred seventy-seven & 10/100 Dollars INV. #1406 Brendan Davis
Lakeside Company 3345 Box 887 Richmond, VA 23173 Sept. 29, 1994 Pay Cypress Products $1,507.77 Fifteen hundred-seven and 77/100 Dollars INV. #1510 Brendan Davis	**Lakeside Company** 3397 Box 887 Richmond, VA 23173 Sept. 29, 1994 Pay Cypress Products $354.05 Three hundred fifty-four and 05/100 Dollars INV. #1616 Brendan Davis

Exhibit 6-5 (continued)

Lakeside Company — 3425 Box 887 Richmond, VA 23173 — Sept 30, 1994 Pay Cypress Products $1,507 77/100 One thousand five hundred-seven and 77/100 Dollars INV. #1691 Brendan Davis	**Lakeside Company** — 3451 Box 887 Richmond, VA 23173 — Oct. 10, 1994 Pay Cypress Products $12,146 73/100 Twelve thousand one hundred forty-six 73/100 Dollars INV. #1812 Brendan Davis
Lakeside Company — 3471 Box 887 Richmond, VA 23173 — Oct. 10, 1994 Pay Cypress Products $2,830 46/100 Two thousand eight hundred-thirty & 46/100 Dollars INV. #2072 Brendan Davis	**Lakeside Company** — 3510 Box 887 Richmond, VA 23173 — Oct. 23, 1994 Pay Cypress Products $14,867 97/100 Fourteen thousand eight hundred sixty-seven & 97/100 Dollars INV. #2149 Brendan Davis

Exhibit 6-6

Cypress Products

MASTER PRICE LIST - PARTIAL
1994

AMPLIFIERS
Model	XY76-R	219.95
	KZ54-T	269.99
	KI34-Z	412.88
	XX99-T	540.00
	BC76-W	688.32

AUDIO COMPONENT SYSTEMS
Model	IU76-R	129.89
	SA36-H	366.00
	JB45-H	481.87
	BM09-H	812.35
	BD17-H	1261.98
	AR65-C	1319.00

CASSETTE TAPE DECKS
Model	CB90-G	62.00
	HG87-X	74.75
	MN78-Z	98.97
	DS45-W	110.50
	CZ55-H	206.98

HEAD PHONES
Model	KJ32-K	32.00
	UH76-E	51.98
	BX08-W	63.22
	PO88-Q	88.97

RADIOS
Model	RA75-L	21.98
	BV24-R	32.30
	ZN56-M	54.99
	IB23-D	88.20
	RA01-O	96.95
	CA35-T	120.00
	CB21-S	181.18

RECEIVERS
Model	FD23-Y	146.99
	LM12-T	234.65
	JB43-A	319.95
	NB73-X	445.70
	CS33-P	698.98

SPEAKERS
Model	WB11-T	56.75
	KM98-G	81.40
	VD34-L	123.40
	YG28-Y	274.95
	BF23-G	469.00

STEREO SYSTEMS
Model	XZ23-U	130.00
	RT45-I	165.98
	VC09-I	210.34
	FU87-R	225.60
	AB15-M	256.98
	ND21-L	285.50
	JH88-A	324.00
	RA69-M	365.00

TURNTABLES
Model	TU62-T	61.00
	NB67-C	85.32
	XW55-P	109.98
	CD00-N	148.50
	RW21-X	165.90
	PH69-D	188.20

COMPACT DISC PLAYERS
Model	CL28-S	109.60
	TL95-R	207.10
	RX04-L	285.99

Exhibit 6-7
Lakeside Company
INVENTORY PURCHASES JOURNAL

Receiving Report	Date	Quantity	Identification #
3918	8-20	20	IB 23-D
		5	HG 87-X
3919	8-21	1	XX 99-T
3920	8-24	1	BM 09-H
		3	LM 12-T
		2	FD 23-Y
3921	8-27	4	YG 28-Y
		2	RT 45-I
		2	FU 87-R
		10	KJ 32-K
		5	BV 24-R
		8	XW 55-P
3922	8-28	1	BD 17-H
		12	KI 34-Z
3923	9-2	6	NB 67-C
		6	XW 55-P
		10	RW 21-X
3924	9-3	30	BV 24-R
		20	RA 01-O
		2	BF 23-G
3925	9-7	1	RA 69-M
3926	9-8	10	KM 98-G
		6	VD 34-L
3927	9-14	5	BC 76-W
		4	BD 17-H
		6	NB 73-X
		2	BF 23-G
		2	XZ 23-U
3928	9-16	1	AR 65-C
		20	PO 88-Q
3929	9-21	60	CB 21-S
		10	NB 73-X

CASE 7

DESIGNING SUBSTANTIVE AUDIT TESTS

Carole Mitchell, supervising senior with the CPA firm of Abernethy and Chapman, is beginning to prepare the final portions of the audit program for the Lakeside Company examination. This program will serve as the guide for substantive tests to be performed on the client's account balances. Mitchell anticipates that these audit procedures will provide the firm with sufficient, competent evidence on which to base an opinion as to the fair presentation of Lakeside's 1994 financial statements.

In designing specific substantive tests for this engagement, Mitchell's judgment has been especially influenced by three factors:

(1) The firm's assessment of inherent risk in the engagement, the possibility, without regards to internal controls, that a material misstatement can occur. This evaluation was based, in part, on a review of the predecessor auditor's working papers, study of the accounting system, discussions with client personnel, and knowledge of the audio equipment industry.

(2) The firm's assessment of control risk, the possibility that a material misstatement would not be prevented or detected on a timely basis by the company's internal control structure. This evaluation was based on gaining an understanding of the control structure, identifying control policies and procedures that would potentially reduce control risk, and testing the controls on which the firm would rely in reducing substantive tests.

(3) Her own analytical procedures performed on the financial information generated by the client during the current year.

Having already completed audit programs for the Revenue and Cash Receipts system as well as Purchases and Cash Disbursements, Mitchell is starting to design substantive testing procedures for Lakeside's payroll balances. She is aware that, except for cost of goods sold, the payroll accounts constitute the largest expense recorded by this client. In 1993, salaries, commissions, bonuses, and payroll taxes amounted to over $1,000,000, and this figure is expected to grow by approximately 7% to 9% in 1994.

Although additional personnel are hired by Lakeside each October, November, and December to handle the Christmas rush, the company normally has 48 employees:

- 11 full-time salaried employees working at Lakeside's office/ warehouse.

- 5 full-time hourly employees working at Lakeside's office/ warehouse.

- 6 full-time sales representatives paid a commission equal to 6.5% of the net sales generated in their territory.

- 6 full-time salaried store managers who participate in a profit-sharing bonus plan.

- 6 full-time salaried assistant store managers who are also included in the profit-sharing bonus arrangement.

- 14 part-time hourly store employees (working an average of 25 hours per week).

Sarah Sweet, employed in the Controller's Division, monitors all of Lakeside's payroll records. Each hourly employee completes a weekly time ticket as a basis for computing gross pay. This ticket must be signed and forwarded to Sweet by the individual's immediate supervisor. In contrast, salaried employees are simply paid 1/12 of their annual salary each month, and sales representatives receive a commission based on their net sales made since the end of the previous pay period.

Sweet completes payroll records for all employees by the tenth day of each month indicating gross wages for the prior period, payroll deductions, and net wages as well as the payroll taxes incurred by Lakeside. A copy of this information is forwarded to Mark Hayes, Controller, who reviews the individual records for reasonableness. If satisfied, he signs the report and routes it to the Treasurer's Office. The payroll is paid on the 15th of every month. On that morning, the Treasurer, Brendan Davis, prepares one check to transfer the total net wages from the general cash fund to the payroll fund. Bob Short, the Assistant Treasurer, then writes individual payroll checks to each employee based on the balances computed by Sweet. These checks are reviewed and signed by the Treasurer, and either delivered or mailed to the employees.

Sweet also maintains all other payroll records required by federal and state laws. She periodically informs the Treasurer's Office of Lakeside's need to make payments for income tax withholding, social security, unemployment taxes, and other related payroll costs.

Having accumulated preliminary data about this payroll system, Mitchell knows that a balance for 1994 of approximately $1.1 million is to be reported as Lakeside's total payroll expense. She plans to corroborate the reported figure through substantive procedures. She begins by identifying potential problems that could prevent the account from being fairly stated. Although she is concerned with all of the broad assertions made by management regarding this account (namely, existence or occurrence, completeness, rights and obligations, valuation or allocation, and presentation and disclosure), she is particularly concerned with the assertions of existence and valuation. For example, she realizes that a Lakeside employee may be receiving his or her own check plus another check made out to a fictitious employee (i.e., problem of existence), or that an hourly employee might be paid for more hours than he or she actually worked (i.e., problem of valuation).

Mitchell plans to pay special attention to the profit-sharing bonus that Lakeside installed during the previous year (1993). To obtain a better understanding of this program, Mitchell talked with Benjamin Rogers, President of Lakeside. He told her that the bonus had been created in an attempt to boost lagging sales in the company's six stores. To stimulate growth, he had decided to offer an annual cash award to each manager and assistant manager based on the net income of their store. This bonus is 4% (2% in 1993 because the plan began in mid-year) of a store's gross profit after subtracting direct salary and rent expenses. The total bonus for each store is then split on a 3 to 1 ratio between the manager and assistant manager. A partially completed worksheet to compute the bonus is included in Exhibit 7-2.

DISCUSSION QUESTIONS

(1) Mitchell seems apprehensive about the bonus system operated by Lakeside. In gathering evidence as to the fair presentation of financial statements, why would an auditor be concerned by such a profit-sharing arrangement?

(2) Since Mitchell is now planning substantive tests, the testing of controls within the payroll system has apparently been completed. This step in the audit process seeks to ascertain control policies and procedures are operating effectively. What specific tests of controls might Mitchell have performed in evaluating this payroll system?

(3) Lakeside is planning to report payroll expense of approximately $1.1 million for 1994. In reporting this figure, the company's management is making assertions encompassing five broad categories: existence or occurrence, completeness, rights and obligations, valuation or allocation, and presentation and disclosure. Explain how each of these assertions relates to the payroll expense balance being reported by Lakeside and give one substantive test that can be used by Abernethy and Chapman to verify each assertion.

(4) A number of evidence gathering techniques, such as observation and confirmation, are available to an auditor in performing audit procedures. The specific methods of gathering evidence depend largely on the type of account in question and the judgment of the auditor. List five additional evidence gathering techniques and indicate the relative significance and reliability of each.

(5) Lakeside maintains a separate bank account for its payroll checks. What benefits are derived from using such a system?

WRITTEN QUESTIONS

(1) Paul Rubens is a new staff auditor recently hired by the firm of Abernethy and Chapman. As one of his initial assignments, he is to perform several audit procedures in the Lakeside engagement. He has already completed a set of payroll tests and prepared the workpaper presented in Exhibit 7-1. The firm of Abernethy and Chapman has a policy that the senior (in-charge) auditor on an engagement must review and approve all such documentation. If errors or problems are found, the workpapers are returned to the staff auditor for appropriate revision. This review process helps to ensure that each workpaper provides a clear and complete indication of the procedures that were performed and the evidence that was accumulated.

Analyze the workpaper in Exhibit 7-1 as if you were the senior auditor. Prepare a list for Reubens of the errors and problems that are present in his workpaper. For each, indicate the reason that the current presentation is not acceptable.

(2) As guidance in designing specific substantive tests, Mitchell is seeking to identify potential problems that might prevent the fair presentation of the client's payroll balance. Prepare a list of these possible problems. In addition, identify a substantive test that Mitchell could perform to ascertain the actuality of each concern.

(3) Because Mitchell is concerned about Lakeside's bonus plan, she has decided to perform a substantive test of the Estimated Bonus Expense (A/C 585). A worksheet is presented in Exhibit 7-2 to aid in this testing. Some of the data were "prepared by the client" but the rest of the worksheet has been given to you to complete. This means that you will have to enter sales and expense data for the nine months ended September 30, 1993 and 1994 from the trial balance in Case 3. You will also need to finish what Mitchell did not have time to complete.

a. Complete the worksheet in Exhibit 7-2. (DISK: CASE7.WKS)

b. Compare the bonus expense you calculated for the nine months ended September 30, 1993 and 1994 with the estimated amount that has been accrued by Lakeside in A/C 585. What is your reaction? What would you suggest?

LIBRARY ASSIGNMENT

(1) Read the following as well as any other published information concerning the auditor's responsibility concerning errors, irregularities and illegal acts committed by the auditor's client:

"The Auditor's New Guide to Errors, Irregularities and Illegal Acts," Journal of Accountancy, September, 1988, p. 40.
"ESM: Implications for the Profession," Journal of Accountancy, April, 1987, p. 94.
"Accountability Standards for Corporate Reporting," Journal of Accountancy, May, 1990, p. 94.
"Illegal Acts: What are the Auditor's Responsibilities?" Journal of Accountancy, January, 1991, p. 82.

This case mentioned several risks involved in performing an audit of the financial statements of Lakeside. One risk is that the client will commit errors, irregularities or illegal acts and the auditor will not detect them. Write a report on the auditor's responsibility for detecting errors, irregularities or illegal acts. What procedures must the auditor perform to detect these? What is management's responsibility? What are the auditor's reporting requirements if any of these are found?

LAKESIDE EXHIBIT 7-1
COMPANY -- PAYROLL TESTS

W/P O-2
PC
12/6/94

May	David Klontz	SM	M-2	Salar.	22,400/yr. ✓	1875- ∅	388- A	97- A	155- ∅	39-	1236- ✓	692-
	John Quinn	SR	M-2	Comm.	6.5% ✓	2316- ∅	479- A	120- A	142- ∅	39-	1536- ✓	702-
	Chad Mitchell	SC	S-1	130 Ⓥ	432/Pw. ✓	546- ∅	102- A	26- A	331- ∅	28-	357- ✓	249-
	Brenda Guthrie	SC	M-3	137 Ⓥ	4.25/hr. ✓	561- ∅	78- A	19- A	34- ∅	49- Ⓐ	381- ✓	690-
	Carol Howell	MAN	M-0	Salar.	24,600/yr. ✓	2150- ∅	523- A	131- A	134- ∅	—	1392- ✓	690-
✓	David Smith	ASM	M-1	Salar.	16,800/yr. ✓	1400- ∅	297- A	74- A	86- ∅	—	943- ✓	704-
Sept.	Bill Drubba	SR	M-5	Comm.	6.5% ✓	1977- ∅	321- A	80- A	121- ∅	69-	1386- ✓	864-
	Karen Steinmuller	ASM	M-4	Salar.	16,200/yr. ✓	1350- ∅	215- A	54- A	83- ∅	63-	935- ✓	Ⓑ
	Jan Luck	MAN	S-1	Salar.	15,900/yr. ✓	1325- ∅	245- A	62- A	81- ∅	—	937- ✓	870-
	John Quinn	SR	M-2	Comm.	6.5% ✓	2541- ∅	526- A	132- A	120- ∅	39-	1844- ✓	878-
	Norman Jackson	SM	M-3	Salar.	23,400/yr. ✓	1950- ∅	295- A	74- A	120- ∅	41-	1420- ✓	869-
	Katrine Baron	ASM	S-1	Salar.	14,700/yr. ✓	1225- ∅	227- A	57- A	75- ∅	29-	838- ✓	861-

Ⓐ Does not appear to agree with rate schedule.
Ⓑ Cancelled checks could not be found.

Ⓥ Compared to time tickets
✓ Verified against company records
∅ Verified calculation
A Checked against government records
✓ Verified extension

Exhibit 7-2
Lakeside Company

Account 585, Estimated Bonus Expense, for Nine Months ended September 30, 1993 and 1994

1993 Bonus Plan

	STORE No.1	STORE No.2	STORE No.3	STORE No.4	STORE No.5	STORE No.6	TOTAL ALL STORES
Sales							
Sales Returns	7,900	25,190	11,950	14,050	30,010	11,300	100,400
Cost of Sales							
Dir. Salary Exp.							
Rent	9,600	28,400	12,000	13,200	30,000	12,000	105,200
Bonus Basis							
x 1993 Bonus %							
BONUS EXPENSE							

Notes: Lakeside makes an "imputed rent" charge to Store No. 6 for the purpose of determining this bonus. Sales (A/C 500); Sales Returns (Prepared by client); Cost of Sales (A/C 550); Direct Salary Expense (A/C 580); Rent (Prepared by client).

Exhibit 7-2 (Cont.)

1994 Bonus Plan

	STORE No. 1	STORE No. 2	STORE No. 3	STORE No. 4	STORE No. 5	STORE No. 6	TOTAL ALL STORES
Sales							
Sales Returns	12,200	29,900	49,500	19,850	8,250	13,700	173,400
Cost of Sales							
Dir. Salary Exp.							
Rent	10,500	33,000	13,200	14,000	32,000	12,000	114,700
Bonus Basis							
x 1994 Bonus %							
BONUS EXPENSE							

See Notes on previous page

CASE 8

OBSERVATION OF PHYSICAL INVENTORY COUNT

The Lakeside Company of Richmond, Virginia takes a physical count of its inventory at the end of each calendar year. The company traditionally carries out this procedure on the first Tuesday in January. Inventory levels are relatively low at this time of year, and Tuesdays are normally very slow days. Each manager and assistant manager normally count the merchandise within their own store while members of Lakeside's inventory department determine the quantity at the company warehouse. Since Lakeside maintains perpetual inventory balances, the final count for every item can be reconciled to the company inventory records as of December 31. All significant variations between the quantity physically present and the perpetual records are double-checked at a later date.

The independent CPA firm of Abernethy and Chapman decides that, because of the material nature of the inventory balances, observation of the January 3, 1995, count will be required. Dan Cline, audit partner for the engagement, suggests that the firm observe the physical inventory taken at the warehouse as well as the count made at two of the company's six stores. These two stores will be selected at random. Wallace Andrews, the audit manager on this engagement, is assigned to discuss the planning of this process with members of the Lakeside management. Because this year's audit is the first for Abernethy and Chapman, Cline wants assurance that the physical inventory procedures are appropriate. Thus, both he and Andrews carefully review a copy of the memo (presented in Exhibit 8-1) which is distributed to all members of the Lakeside counting team. This memo is designed to ensure that all personnel understand fully the tasks that they are to perform.

As can be seen from the memo in Exhibit 8-1, Lakeside utilizes a "tag system" for counting inventory. Prior to the actual count, the inventory is separated into groups of like items. Employees then complete and attach a prenumbered tag (see Exhibit 8-2) to each group. This tag includes a description of the merchandise and the quantity present. Later, after all of the inventory has been counted and tagged, the lower portion of each tag is detached and returned to the Controller's Office for listing. This list provides Lakeside with a record of all merchandise presently being held. Subsequently, the Controller's Office inserts a unit cost for each of these items. The total cost is then computed by multiplying the quantity times the unit cost. These individual amounts are added to arrive at the gross cost of the January 3 ending inventory. Lakeside still has to "roll" this figure back to the December 31 balance by removing the effects of any January 1 and January 2 transactions. As the final step in this process, the December 31 adjusted total must be reduced by any discounts taken in acquiring the current merchandise. The resulting balance will be reported as the cost of Lakeside's inventory.

Carole Mitchell has been assigned by Abernethy and Chapman to observe the physical inventory taken at the client's warehouse. Prior to January 3, she reviews Lakeside's physical inventory memo (Exhibit 8-1) to provide herself with an understanding of the process being used. On that Tuesday morning, Mitchell arrives just before 8:00 A.M. and begins her work by discussing the counting procedures with the Lakeside employees who are present. She then proceeds to the inventory department's files and locates all receiving reports and bills of lading for the past week. She records these document numbers and their dates as well as the quantity and description of the merchandise received and shipped.

When Mitchell returns to the actual count, she has several specific audit tasks to perform:

(1) She verifies that the tags are consecutively numbered.

(2) She observes and evaluates the reliability of the procedures being utilized by the client. Lakeside uses a two-person system whereby one individual counts the inventory while the other records the relevant information on the tags. Mitchell makes certain that all employees understand their tasks and are following the instructions properly.

(3) She examines the client's inventory for any sign of damage, obsolescence, or other problems that would prevent the merchandise from being sold at normal prices.

(4) She searches for any evidence that might disclose inventory items being held on consignment or that for some other reason did not belong to Lakeside.

(5) She also searches for inventory that is hidden or overlooked in the counting process.

(6) After all items have been counted and tagged, she records the last tag number that was used.

(7) On a sample basis, she counts the inventory actually present to ascertain that this quantity agrees with the figure listed on the tag. She records each of these test counts in her work papers.

(8) She authorizes the employees to collect the inventory tags.

After Mitchell completes her inventory observation, she documents her findings in the work paper presented in Exhibit 8-3. Several days later, she receives a complete listing of the company's inventory from Lakeside. The portion relating to the warehouse count is reproduced in Exhibit 8-4. This inventory has been costed using a Master Price List furnished by Cypress Products (see Exhibit 6-6). As can be seen at the bottom of Exhibit 8-4, Lakeside has already adjusted the total count for inventory transactions occurring on January 1 and January 2. Further reduction is made for the 3% cash discount available from Cypress as well as monthly discounts offered on selected items. Thus, the physical inventory in the warehouse as of December 31, 1994 had a cost to Lakeside of $665,997.57. On that same date, the company's perpetual records indicated a balance of $672,154.35 so that a year-end reduction of $6,156.78 is necessary to reconcile the accounting records with the inventory count.

DISCUSSION QUESTIONS

(1) Why would the physical count of Lakeside's inventory produce a balance more than $6,000 below the figure indicated by the company's own perpetual records? Is this difference a material amount that warrants further investigation by Abernethy and Chapman?

(2) Members of a company's management may occasionally attempt to overcount ending inventory. What is the rationale behind this type of irregularity? Is this potential problem especially significant in the audit of the Lakeside stores?

(3) Members of a company's management may occasionally attempt to undercount ending inventory. What is the rationale behind this type of irregularity? Is this potential problem especially significant in the audit of the Lakeside stores?

(4) Assume that a material misstatement occurs (either unintentionally or otherwise) in counting Lakeside's inventory. The problem is not discovered by Abernethy and Chapman and eventually appears within the client's financial statements. What is the CPA firm's responsibility for such misstatements?

(5) The CPA firm of Abernethy and Chapman has decided to observe the physical inventory at only two of Lakeside's six stores. Given the materiality of the inventory balance, was this decision appropriate?

(6) As part of the substantive testing of inventory balances, the auditor normally reviews the client's sales returns for the period immediately following the end of the fiscal year. What is the significance of this testing procedure?

(7) In her observation, Mitchell recorded the last inventory tag number used by Lakeside. What is the significance of this testing procedure?

(8) What actions should Mitchell have taken if she had discovered any damaged or obsolete inventory items?

(9) Evaluate the effectiveness and efficiency of Lakeside's physical inventory procedures.

WRITTEN QUESTIONS

(1) Mitchell wants to verify that the inventory listing shown in Exhibit 8-4 agrees with the physical count she observed and that it provides a fairly presented inventory cost balance. She assigns this task to Paul Reubens, a new staff auditor recently hired by the firm of Abernethy and Chapman. Prepare a step-by-step audit program for Reubens so that he can perform this substantive testing. If a sample is to be drawn (and no specification as to size is indicated), select a sample of 8 items.

(2) Carry out the audit program designed in Number (1) above. Prepare a work paper to document the procedures that were performed and the evidence gathered. When specified tests cannot be completed, describe the steps that should have been taken. Indicate whether $665,997.57 should be accepted as a fairly presented representation of the inventory held in Lakeside's warehouse. (DISK: CASE8.WKS)

Exhibit 8-1

Lakeside Company
INTERCOMPANY MEMO

TO: All Store Managers, All Assistant Store Managers, All Members of the Inventory Department

FROM: Edward Thomas, Vice-President

SUBJECT: Annual Physical Inventory

DATE: December 2, 1994

We will count the inventory at all of the Lakeside stores as well as the warehouse on Tuesday, January 3, 1995. Each of the store managers will be responsible for the physical inventory at their store. The inventory department will count the merchandise here at the warehouse. You should plan to perform the following steps:

PRELIMINARY

(1) During the week prior to the 3rd, ship out all inventory that has been sold so that it will not be accidentally counted.

(2) Isolate and label any inventory that does not belong to Lakeside. These items will include merchandise returned for repair as well as sold inventory that could not be shipped out at this time.

(3) Isolate and label any damaged inventory or other items where marketability has been impaired.

(4) Group similar inventory items. Counting will be easier and quicker if, for example, all radios of a particular type are already together.

(5) Make certain that you have enough prenumbered inventory tags. These tags should be picked up at the warehouse by Friday afternoon. You should have at least 200 tags. Verify that the numbers are sequential and that no numbers are missing.

(6) Inform all employees who will be assisting in the count of their responsibilities. Give each of these employees a copy of this memo and ask them to read it prior to the 3rd.

Counting Procedures

(1) Have all employees arrive by 8:00 A.M. on Tuesday, January 3. We normally assume that two people can count a store's entire

inventory in about 4 to 6 hours. Eight people will be needed to count the warehouse inventory. You may ask more employees to assist but remember that they must be paid overtime wage rates.

(2) A member of the auditing firm of Abernethy and Chapman may be present to observe your count. If an auditor is on hand, this individual should be given full cooperation and allowed to perform any procedures considered necessary.

(3) Divide the employees into two member counting teams. Before the actual count begins, review all instructions with each team.

(4) One member of each team should count the inventory while the other records the quantity, the type of item, and the Cypress serial number on a prenumbered inventory tag. The tag should then be attached at a prominent place on the inventory items. Tags must be used sequentially.

(5) All tags should be completed in ink. If a change needs to be made to a tag, the original data should be marked out and the correction entered. The person making the alteration must initial the change. To ensure that unauthorized changes are not made, no erasures are permitted.

(6) If any tags have to be voided, write "VOID" across the face. These tags should be saved and returned with the unused tags.

(7) Each team is responsible for counting all inventory within the assigned areas. Any items not counted should be clearly labelled, giving the reasons for exclusion.

(8) When a team has counted and tagged all inventory, the person in charge of the count should be informed (as well as the auditor if present).

(9) The in-charge employee will examine the area to ensure that all merchandise is tagged. The auditor should be allowed to perform whatever tests are considered necessary. After both the in-charge employee and the auditor have completed their review, the counting team will return and remove the bottom portion of each tag.

(10) The counting team sorts the tags into numerical order making certain that all tags are present. When all tags are located, the in-charge employee should bring them directly to the company office and give them to me on Sunday afternoon.

(11) If any problems arise, call me at the company office immediately.

Exhibit 8-2
Lakeside Company
SAMPLE - INVENTORY TAG

```
           INVENTORY TAG

              No. 101
- - - - - - - - - - - - - - - - - - - - - -
              No. 101


   Item Description:  _____
   _____

   Serial Number:    _____

   Quantity:         _____

   Unit of Measure:  _____


   Counted By:       _____

   Checked By:       _____


              No. 101
```

EXHIBIT 8-3

LAKESIDE COMPANY -- RECEIVING & SHIPPING INVENTORY CUT-OFF
DECEMBER 31, 1994

W. P. No.	F-1
Accountant	CM
Date	1/3/95

I. Receiving Reports (week of 12/28/94 – 1/2/95)

Date	Item	R.R. #	Serial #	Quantity
12/28/94	Radios	3987	IB 23-D	75
12/28/94	Speakers	3987	VD 34-L	40
12/28/94	Amplifiers	3987	KZ 54-T	50
1/1/95	Component Systems	3988	JB 45-H	20
1/2/95	Head Phones	3989	KJ 32-K	40
1/2/95	Compact Disc Players	3989	RX 04-L	10

II. Bills of Lading (week of 12/28/94 – 1/2/95)

Date	Item	Shipped to	B.L. #	Serial #	Quantity
12/28/94	Component Systems	Customer	6012	SA 36-H	5
12/28/94	Radios	Customer	6013	ZN 56-M	20
12/30/94	Amplifiers	Store 4	6014	XX 99-T	5
12/30/94	Amplifiers	Store 4	6014	BC 76-W	4
1/1/95	Amplifiers	Customer	6015	XY 76-R	20
1/1/95	Component Systems	Customer	6015	BM 09-H	10
1/2/95	Stereo Systems	Customer	6016	AB 15-M	20
1/2/95	Stereo Systems	Customer	6016	JH 88-A	12
1/2/95	Receivers	Customer	6016	CS 33-P	10
1/2/95	Component Systems	Customer	6016	AR 65-C	6
1/2/95	Speakers	Store 1	6017	BF 23-G	8

Inventory Tag Count and Procedures

- Lakeside uses a tag system in counting inventory. Each team member appeared to understand and follow company procedures.

- Counting Teams Were:
  1. Stan Wisdom   2. David Stockman   3. Edward Thomas   4. Jeff Mullins
     Ralph Lewis   Ron Livingston   Chad Nance   Bob Simon

- Tags #101-300 assigned to warehouse. All tags reviewed and found to be consecutively numbered. Last tag used: #152. All tags (#101-152) were pulled and accounted for.

EXHIBIT 8-3 (Continued)
LAKESIDE COMPANY -- PHYSICAL INVENTORY TEST COUNTS — WAREHOUSE
DECEMBER 31, 1994

W/P F-2
CM
1/3/94

INVENTORY ITEMS	TAG NO.	SERIAL NO.	QUANTITY
Amplifiers	116	BC 76-W	22
Component Systems	124	JB 45-H	69
Radios	102	CB 21-S	80
Stereo Systems	138	FU 87-R	60 Ⓐ
Amplifiers	130	KZ 54-T	88
Speakers	150	YG 28-Y	71
Stereo Systems	127	RA 69-M	99
Turntables	142	RW 21-X	49
Receivers	113	NB 73-X	112
Stereo Systems	126	JH 88-A	77
Tape Decks	104	CZ 55-H	46
Speakers	137	BF 23-G	84
Head Phones	147	PO 88-Q	49
Turntables	132	CD 00-N	121

Ⓐ Lakeside's count was adjusted from 59 to 60.

Several items did not belong to Lakeside. They had been returned for repairs or adjustment and a properly completed "Repair Memo" was on hand signed by the customer and a Lakeside representative. These items did not appear to have a value of over $1,000.

Audit Objective:

To gather evidence of inventory existence and to assure that it was counted accurately. To verify that unsalable merchandise is excluded and imperfect items are appropriately earmarked.

Audit Conclusion:

All items (except Ⓐ above) correctly counted with no items missing, or omitted. No damaged or obsolete inventory was observed in the warehouse.

Exhibit 8-4

Lakeside Company

PHYSICAL INVENTORY - WAREHOUSE

January 3, 1995   Page 1 of 3

TAG NUMBER	DESCRIPTION	SERIAL NUMBER	QUAN- TITY	COST/UNIT	TOTAL COST
101	Radios	BV24-R	68	32.30	2,196.40
102	Radios	CB21-S	80	181.18	14,494.40
103	Tape Decks	CB90-G	125	62.00	7,750.00
104	Tape Decks	CZ55-H	46	206.98	9,521.08
105	Radios	CA35-T	61	120.00	7,320.00
106	Receivers	JB43-A	77	319.95	24,636.15
107	Receivers	LM12-T	105	234.65	24,638.25
108	Receivers	CS33-P	6	698.98	4,193.88
109	Radios	RA01-O	139	96.95	13,476.05
110	Radios	IB23-D	128	88.20	11,289.60
111	Amplifiers	XY76-R	48	219.95	10,557.60
112	Receivers	FD23-Y	86	146.99	12,641.14
113	Receivers	NB73-X	112	445.70	49,918.40
114	Component Systems	SA36-H	2	366.00	732.00
115	Amplifiers	XX99-T	29	540.00	15,660.00
116	Amplifiers	BC76-W	22	688.32	15,143.04
117	Component Systems	AR65-C	2	1,319.00	2,638.00
118	Component Systems	BD17-H	52	1,261.98	65,622.96
119	Component Systems	IU76-R	22	129.89	2,857.58
120	Radios	RA75-L	146	21.98	3,209.08
121	Radios	ZN56-M	89	54.99	4,894.11
122	Speakers	VD34-L	85	123.40	10,489.00
123	Speakers	WB11-T	47	56.75	2,667.25
124	Component Systems	JB45-H	69	481.87	33,249.03
125	Component Systems	BM09-H	3	812.35	2,437.05
126	Stereo Systems	JH88-A	77	324.00	24,948.00
127	Stereo Systems	RA69-M	99	365.00	36,135.00
128	Stereo Systems	XZ23-U	62	130.00	8,060.00
129	Stereo Systems	VC09-I	46	210.34	9,675.64
130	Amplifiers	KZ54-T	88	269.99	23,759.12

Exhibit 8-4 (Continued)

Lakeside Company

PHYSICAL INVENTORY - WAREHOUSE

January 3, 1995   Page 2 of 3

TAG NUMBER	DESCRIPTION	SERIAL NUMBER	QUAN-TITY	COST/UNIT	TOTAL COST
131	Amplifiers	KI34-Z	26	412.88	10,734.88
132	Turntables	CD00-N	121	148.50	17,968.50
133	Stereo Systems	RT45-I	5	165.98	829.90
134	Turntables	PH69-D	2	188.20	376.40
135	Stereo Systems	ND21-L	104	285.50	29,692.00
136	Stereo Systems	AB15-M	36	256.98	9,251.28
137	Speakers	BF23-G	84	469.00	39,396.00
138	Stereo Systems	FU87-R	60	225.60	13,536.00
139	Turntables	TU62-T	87	61.00	5,307.00
140	Turntables	NB67-C	4	85.32	341.28
141	Head Phones	BX08-W	98	63.22	6,195.56
142	Turntables	RW21-X	49	165.90	8,129.10
143	Tape Decks	HG87-X	127	74.75	9,493.25
144	Tape Decks	DS45-W	114	110.50	12,597.00
145	Tape Decks	MN78-Z	11	98.97	1,088.67
146	Turntables	XW55-P	76	109.98	8,358.48
147	Head Phones	PO88-Q	49	88.97	4,359.53
148	Head Phones	KJ32-K	143	32.00	4,576.00
149	Speakers	KM98-G	66	81.40	5,372.40
150	Speakers	YG28-Y	71	274.95	19,521.45
151	Head Phones	UH76-E	3	51.98	155.94
152	Compact Disc Players	RX04-L	10	285.99	2,859.90

TOTAL COST OF INVENTORY - JANUARY 3, 1995 - WAREHOUSE $664,950.33

Exhibit 8-4 (Continued)

Lakeside Company

PHYSICAL INVENTORY - WAREHOUSE

January 3, 1995   Page 3 of 3

TOTAL COST OF INVENTORY - JANUARY 3, 1995 - WAREHOUSE	$664,950.33
Less: Inventory Received on January 1 and January 2 (from Receiving Reports)	(13,777.30)
Add: Inventory Shipped Out on January 1 and January 2 (from Bills of Lading)	40,205.90
TOTAL COST OF INVENTORY - DECEMBER 31, 1994 - WAREHOUSE	$691,378.93
Less: Adjustments for Monthly Discounts Given by Cypress	
Tag 113 - Discount $30.00 x 85 Items Purchased	(2,550.00)
Tag 121 - Discount $ 8.25 x 40 Items Purchased	(330.00)
Tag 132 - Discount $12.60 x 60 Items Purchased	(756.00)
Tag 146 - Discount $11.50 x 80 Items Purchased	(920.00)
Tag 149 - Discount $ 6.50 x 35 Items Purchased	(227.50)
SUB-TOTAL	$686,595.43
Less: Adjustment for 3% Cash Discount Taken on All Inventory Purchases	(20,597.86)
TOTAL ADJUSTED COST OF INVENTORY - DECEMBER 31, 1994 - WAREHOUSE	$665,997.57
INVENTORY IN WAREHOUSE PER PERPETUAL INVENTORY RECORDS	(672,154.35)
INVENTORY ADJUSTMENT (REDUCTION)	$(6,156.78)

CASE 9

RESOLVING AUDIT PROBLEMS

Early in 1995, Wallace Andrews, manager with the CPA firm of Abernethy and Chapman, visited the headquarters of the Lakeside Company. Andrews was making a periodic review of the audit work performed to date by Carole Mitchell, Art Heyman, and Paul Reubens. He also wanted to discuss the examination with Benjamin Rogers, president of Lakeside. During every engagement, Abernethy and Chapman auditors attempt to keep the client's senior management advised of the progress being made. In addition, several matters had been brought to Andrews' attention that he felt should be discussed with Rogers.

The first of these issues concerned a major addition being made to the company warehouse. In reading the minutes of the Board of Directors' meetings (see Exhibit 9-1), Andrews had noted the Board's approval of a $220,000 expansion and renovation to this facility. Early in December, Andrews inspected the actual construction work which was approximately one-fourth complete at that time. Then, at year-end, a bank confirmation was mailed to the Virginia Capital Security Bank, the organization financing the project (see Exhibit 9-2). The completed confirmation returned by the bank indicated that Lakeside had borrowed $100,000 to date.

When asked about the construction, Rogers described Lakeside's negotiation of a $200,000 mortgage loan to finance the expansion. The cash was to be provided to the company in four equal monthly installments beginning on November 15. According to Rogers, "This entire construction project, both the addition and the renovation, should be finished by March 1, 1995. Although we can't be sure of the total cost just yet, it should be approximately $225,000. We will use Lakeside's own funds to finance costs over and above the $200,000 loan. We borrowed the money from Virginia Capital at a 10% rate. I talked to a number of other banks and lenders but that was the best rate that was available at the time."

Several potential accounting problems involving the expansion concerned Andrews. First, he was worried that Lakeside might already be recording depreciation expense on the addition even though it was not yet in operation. Rogers assumed that the company's method of accounting was correct but suggested that Andrews discuss the handling of this matter with the controller.

Andrews also wanted to verify that Lakeside was properly capitalizing the interest costs incurred during the construction as required by Statement 34 of the Financial Accounting Standards Board. Rogers confessed that he knew nothing about this particular accounting pronouncement. He was virtually certain, though, that

Lakeside would have expensed any interest on the debt. However, no interest charges had yet been paid or recorded in connection with the project. Rogers suggested that the audit team calculate an appropriate adjustment to capitalize this interest for the current period.

Andrews' final concern in auditing the warehouse expansion involved Lakeside's method of separating repair expenses from capitalized costs. The Board of Directors' minutes had indicated that the old warehouse facility was to be repaired as part of the construction work. Andrews was interested in the procedures being used by the company to isolate these repair costs. Rogers replied that no special techniques had been incorporated to account for the construction project. As with all expenditures, except for inventory purchases which were handled separately, invoices were "coded" by the Controller's Office upon receipt. This process required each invoice to be stamped and an account number written in to identify the appropriate debit entry for the transaction. Thus, all invoices were reviewed and classified at that time to separate capital expenditures from repair expenses. Rogers stated that his signature was also necessary on all invoices that required a payment of over $200, but he made no attempt to verify the accuracy of the account coding.

Andrews then moved the discussion to the issue of the seventh store which Lakeside had begun operating on December 1, 1994, in Williamsburg, Virginia. Carole Mitchell had informed Andrews that a $21,000 payment was made by Lakeside on November 28, 1994, to Rogers Development Company, the corporation which constructed this building and was leasing it to Lakeside. She also revealed that Rogers Development Company was owned by Benjamin Rogers and his wife. The entire $21,000 had been charged by Lakeside to a Prepaid Rent account with 1/12 of this total being subsequently reclassified to Rent Expense for the month of December. Andrews was very concerned as to whether this rental agreement constituted a capitalized lease based on the criteria established by Statement 13 of the Financial Accounting Standards Board.

Rogers adamantly refused to even entertain the possibility that this arrangement might be a capital lease. He immediately brought out the rental contract (see Exhibit 9-3) between Lakeside and his construction company. "The agreement is for one year only. We will renegotiate on a year-by-year basis; the Board of Directors fully agrees with the handling of this matter. In addition, the price is quite reasonable for that store at that location. I even checked into this matter with a lawyer before drawing up the contract. Neither a bargain purchase option nor a transfer of ownership is included in the lease. The building has a useful life of at least 25 years; thus, the one-year contract is for a period of time less than 75% of the property's economic life. Finally, since the residual value is not guaranteed, the $21,000 payment fails to satisfy the 90% present value criterion. This lease simply does not meet any test for being a capital lease."

Andrews was quite surprised by Rogers' fervor. Upon further questioning, the president indicated that "growth is important to me. To grow, Lakeside has to be able to borrow money and, thus, needs a good debt/equity ratio. By financing the building in this manner, the construction debt is actually mine and not that of the company. I plan to earn a reasonable return on my investment but, even more importantly, Lakeside maintains its borrowing potential. I do realize that this lease qualifies as a related party transaction and will have to be disclosed in a note to the financial statements. However, I'm not sure that anyone actually reads those notes."

Andrews was concerned by Rogers' contentions and decided to discuss the issue with Dan Cline, the audit partner on the engagement, before taking further action. He also wanted to read Statement 13 once again to see if any guidance was offered by the pronouncement. Thus, he chose to forego additional discussion with Rogers concerning the lease and moved to his final agenda item: Lakeside's Store 6.

Store 6 first began operations in November of 1992 but had never proven successful. The previous audit firm had even added a paragraph to its opinion on Lakeside's 1993 financial statements because of the uncertainty surrounding the company's ability to recover this investment. Although sales were up slightly in 1994, the store continued to show a considerable loss after two years of operation. The adjacent shopping center was still having its own problems, with less than 60% of the available space being rented. Andrews did not believe that Store 6 was capable of generating a profit in the foreseeable future.

When questioned, Rogers was somewhat philosophical about the situation. "We studied that market before we went into it. We felt that the location had long-range potential and we still do. Lakeside is not the kind of company that enters an area on an impulse and then pulls up stakes if things don't go our way at first. We can make that store profitable and we will. I wasted too much time last year arguing with King and Company over this issue. As you know, that firm is gone and the store is still at the shopping center making sales. Store 6 will be doing business for as long as Lakeside is in business. I really have nothing further to say on the matter."

DISCUSSION QUESTIONS

(1)   Why would a company's principal officer not know about an important accounting pronouncement such as Statement 34 of the FASB?

(2)   Why is depreciation expense not recorded until after an asset is put into use?

(3) Rogers suggested that Abernethy and Chapman calculate the amount of interest that should be capitalized this year for the construction project. Since the financial statements are the responsibility of the management, is this action appropriate for an audit engagement?

(4) What should Andrews do now concerning the lease arrangement that has been created for the seventh store? Will Lakeside's financial statements be fairly presented if this lease is reported as an operating lease rather than a capitalized lease? Is inclusion within the notes to the financial statements an adequate way of reporting this lease?

(5) Why are related party transactions separately disclosed in financial statement notes?

(6) Despite Rogers' assurances, Store 6 could still be closed down, resulting in a large loss to Lakeside. An uncertainty paragraph was added to the audit opinion in the previous year and the situation has not changed significantly. Should Abernethy and Chapman give a similar opinion this year to protect themselves from potential liability?

(7) What should Abernethy and Chapman do now in connection with the uncertainty involved with Store 6?

(8) When Rogers made reference to the firing of King and Company, was he issuing a threat to the current auditors?

WRITTEN QUESTION

(1) Following his discussion with Rogers, Andrews talked briefly with Carole Mitchell concerning the warehouse expansion. She indicated that Art Heyman had already prepared an analysis of the Repairs and Maintenance account (see Exhibit 9-4). In addition, based on the debits to the Warehouse account (see Exhibit 9-5), he had located the invoices substantiating the capitalized transactions (see Exhibit 9-6). Two other related invoices (see Exhibit 9-7) were discovered by the audit team while reviewing the invoices received by Lakeside subsequent to the end of 1994.

Analyze the Warehouse account in a manner similar to that used by Heyman for the Repairs and Maintenance account. Indicate on the work paper any proposed correcting entries that are needed to ensure fair presentation of this financial information. (DISK: CASE9.DOC)

LIBRARY ASSIGNMENT

(1) Read the following as well as other published information concerning the auditor's evaluation of an entity's ability to continue as a going concern:

"SAS No. 59: How to Evaluate Going Concern," Journal of Accountancy, January, 1989, p. 24.
"Documenting Compliance with SAS 59," CPA Journal, July, 1989, p. 50.
"Understanding SAS No. 59: The Auditor's Going Concern Responsibilities," Practical Accountant, September, 1989, p. 50.
"What Do Auditors Really Consider in Making Going-Concern Judgments?" Practical Accountant, August, 1990, p. 64.
"Going...Going...Gone," CA Magazine, April, 1991, p. 22.

In this case, the accounting firm of Abernethy and Chapman is considering the potential of Lakeside's Store 6 to continue as a viable operation. Under Statement on Auditing Standards No. 59, auditors must consider the entire entity's ability to continue as a going concern. Write a report discussing the auditor's responsibilities under SAS 59. What do auditors consider in evaluating the going concern question? What difficulties might an auditor encounter in making this evaluation?

Exhibit 9-1

Lakeside Company
MINUTES - BOARD OF DIRECTORS' MEETING
September 1, 1994

Meeting was called to order at 1:00 P.M.
Members present: Benjamin Rogers, Scott Arnold, Steve Reese, and Bob Verga
Members absent: None

Rogers distributed Lakeside's interim financial information for the first two quarters of 1994 and discussed the major changes in results from the previous year. Questions followed concerning specific revenue and expense items. Discussion centered on methods for increasing store sales, especially at Store 6. Rogers stated that he was confident the new bonus incentive system would generate additional sales by encouraging the management of each store to be more aggressive.

Rogers offered a motion that a $15,000 cash dividend be paid to the owners on record as of September 10. The motion was seconded by Verga, with discussion following. Rogers explained that the dividend was less than the previous year but that the company needed to maintain a strong liquidity position to ensure growth. This motion passed unanimously.

Rogers indicated that the seventh Lakeside store would be opening on or about December 1 to take advantage of the Christmas rush. The store is being built in Williamsburg, Virginia by Rogers Development Company, a company wholly owned by Rogers and his wife. Rogers offered a motion that Lakeside sign a one-year lease for this property beginning on December 1, 1994, at a price of $21,000 per year to be paid in advance. Verga seconded this motion and discussion followed. Reese asked for an explanation for having Rogers construct the facility instead of Lakeside. The president indicated that this arrangement was designed to protect the debt/equity ratio of the company. This motion passed unanimously.

Rogers offered a motion that $200,000 be borrowed to build an addition to the company warehouse as well as to renovate the present facility. The motion was seconded by Arnold and considerable discussion followed. Rogers stated that the warehouse roof needed immediate repair because leaks were endangering the inventory. At the same time, because of the increased growth of distributorship sales, the facility no longer would hold an adequate supply of merchandise. Rogers said that he had already received an estimate of $220,000 for both fixing the roof and increasing the size of the warehouse by approximately one-half.

Of this amount, Lakeside would borrow $200,000 and put up the rest from current funds. Concern was expressed because of the high interest rates being charged at the present time. Reese suggested that Rogers talk with several lenders in order to obtain the lowest possible rate. This motion passed unanimously.

Meeting adjourned at 2:40 P.M.

_____
Steve Reese, Secretary

EXHIBIT 9-2
STANDARD BANK CONFIRMATION INQUIRY
Approved 1966 by
AMERICAN INSTITUTE OF CERTIFIED PUBLIC ACCOUNTANTS
NABAC, THE ASSOCIATION FOR BANK AUDIT, CONTROL AND OPERATION

ORIGINAL — To be retained by Bank

December 31, 1994

Your completion of the following report will be sincerely appreciated. IF THE ANSWER TO ANY ITEM IS "NONE", PLEASE SO STATE. Kindly mail it in the enclosed stamped, addressed envelope *direct* to the accountant named below.

Report from (Bank): Virginia Capital Security Bank, Box 9861, Richmond, Va. 23219

Yours truly, Lakeside Company (Account Name Per Bank Records)
By Brendan Davis, Treasurer (Authorized Signature)

Bank customer should check here if confirmation of bank balances only (item 1) is desired. ☐

NOTE—If the space provided is inadequate, please enter totals hereon and attach a statement giving full details as called for by the columnar headings below.

To: Abernethy and Chapman, CPAs
James Center -- Suite 1430
Richmond, Va. 23219

1. At the close of business on DECEMBER 31, 1994 our records showed the following balance(s) to the *credit* of the above named customer. In the event that we could readily ascertain whether there were any balances to the credit of the customer not designated in this request, the appropriate information is given below:

AMOUNT	ACCOUNT NAME	ACCOUNT NUMBER	SUBJECT TO WITHDRAWAL BY CHECK?	INTEREST BEARING? GIVE RATE
$ none				

2. The customer was directly liable to us in respect of loans, acceptances, etc., at the close of business on that date in the total amount of $ 100,000—, as follows:

AMOUNT	DATE OF LOAN OR DISCOUNT	DUE DATE	INTEREST RATE	PAID TO	DESCRIPTION OF LIABILITY, COLLATERAL, SECURITY INTERESTS, LIENS, ENDORSERS, ETC.
$100,000	11/15/94 12/15/94	12/31/99	10%	—	Lien on warehouse

3. The customer was contingently liable as endorser of notes discounted and/or as guarantor at the close of business on that date in the total amount of $ none, as below:

AMOUNT	NAME OF MAKER	DATE OF NOTE	DUE DATE	REMARKS
$ none				

4. Other direct or contingent liabilities, open letters of credit, and relative collateral, were
none

5. Security agreements under the Uniform Commercial Code or any other agreements providing for restrictions, not noted above, were as follows (if officially recorded, indicate date and office in which filed):
none

Date January 6, 1995

Yours truly, (Bank) VIRGINIA CAPITAL SECURITY
By Elaine Wilson, Customer Service
Authorized Signature

FORM WP-681 (REV. 10/66)

Exhibit 9-3

RENTAL AGREEMENT

The following shall constitute a legal agreement between Rogers Development Company ("Lessor") and the Lakeside Company ("Lessee") as to the leasing of land and building ("Property") located at 910 Second Street in Williamsburg, Virginia.

The agreements between the Lessor and the Lessee are as follows:

(1) The lease shall run from December 1, 1994 through November 30, 1995.

(2) The Lessee shall deliver to the Lessor a payment of $21,000 prior to the initial lease date as stated above. This payment shall give the Lessee sole privilege to use the Property for the period of time of the lease.

(3) All utilities, property taxes, and maintenance costs associated with the Property for the period of the lease shall be the sole responsibility of the Lessee.

(4) Any permanent improvements of the property shall be the sole responsibility of the Lessee subject to prior written approval of the Lessor. Any attachments to the Property shall become the property of the Lessor subject to the laws of the Commonwealth of Virginia.

(5) The Lessee makes no guarantee as to the value of the Property at the end of the lease period but does guarantee to repair any physical damage to the Property.

(6) The Lessor agrees to maintain adequate insurance coverage on the Property while the Lessee agrees to maintain adequate insurance coverage on the contents therein.

LESSOR: LESSEE:
ROGERS DEVELOPMENT COMPANY   **LAKESIDE COMPANY**

BY:_____   BY: _____

DATE: _____   DATE: _____

EXHIBIT 9-4

W. P. No. X-1
ACCOUNT JH
DATE 1/16/95

LAKESIDE COMPANY
A/C 640-1, REPAIRS AND MAINTENANCE
12/31/94

Invoice No.	Vendor	Invoice Date	Dollar Amount	Audit Procedures	Comments
2891	Barnes Lumber Co.	2/8/94	912.32	√ ✗	Repaired loading dock at Store 3.
2932	Jackson Tile	3/19/94	882.19	√ ✗	Retiled rest room at office Ⓐ
2978	Gainer Electrical	5/11/94	3142.91	√Ⓑ✗	Rewiring of electrical system in Store 6; storm damage.
2989	Bones Ford	5/9/94	1606.93	√ ✗	Repair company trucks; accident damage Ⓒ
3011	Davis Paving	6/1/94	8086.00	√ ✗	Paving and landscaping around store 6 Ⓒ
3030	Bones Ford	6/13/94	81069	√ ✗	Repair of 3 trucks.
3052	Richmond Paint Co.	7/5/94	1200.00	√ ✗	Repaint company office.
3069	DZ Advertising	7/11/94	11500.00	√ ✗	Advertising for May and June Ⓓ
3106	Harper Roofing	9/1/94	1180.00	√ ✗	Roof repair for warehouse.
3125	Southside Shopping Center	9/20/94	15647.25	√ ✗	Renovation of Store 2 Ⓔ
3144	Davis Paving	10/6/94	3123.41	√ ✗	Repair warehouse parking lot.
3192	Freeman Office Equipment	11/10/94	848.00	√ ✗	Overhaul office equipment.
3209	Harper Roofing	12/2/94	612.00	√ ✗	Roof repair for warehouse.
2950	Seymour Total Collection	4/9/94	175.00	√ ✗	Haul away debris from warehouse repair.
3081	Richmond Cleaning Service	7/30/94	240.00	√ ✗	Cleaning for Stores 2, 3 and 4.
3099	Bones Ford	8/6/94	62.35	√ ✗	Tune-up of company truck.
3159	Seymour Trash Collection	10/20/94	175.00	∅ ∧	Trash Collection *
*Various	87 other payments under $500	Various	5349.62		
	Total per General Ledger @ 12/31/94		53367.60		
	Proposed adjustment Ⓒ Ⓓ		⟨8086.00⟩		
	Proposed adjustment		⟨11500.00⟩		
	Adjusted total		33781.60		

Audit Procedures:
√ Traced to purchase invoice. Noted agreement as to amount and date, except Ⓑ.
✗ Examined purchase invoice for proper authorization.
✗ Verified mathematical accuracy of invoice.
∅ Traced to General Ledger posting.
∧ Verified footing & ledger account.

Audit Objective: To verify that expenditures are legitimate repair and maintenance costs, property classified, and that no portion should be capitalized.

Audit Conclusion: The account appears fairly stated Ⓒ Ⓓ Ⓔ and pending Ⓔ in accordance with GAAP, after adjustments.

Scope:
Population: All charges to Repair and Maintenance A/C 640-1.
Sample: Judgmental: All expenditures over $500 and 10% of those less than $500, picked at random.

NOTES

Ⓐ Discussed work with Edward Thomas. Appears the legitimate expense.
Ⓑ Invoice was for $3600. Lakeside suffered bill but it was reduced by Gainer Electrical to $3142.91. Reasonable correspondence. Appears legitimate.
Ⓒ Paving and landscaping should be capitalized:

PROPOSED ADJUSTMENT

Land Improvement 8086—
  Repairs and Maintenance 8086—

Ⓓ Apparent coding error. Advertising expense is AC 600-1.
PROPOSED ADJUSTMENT
Advertising Expense 11500—
  Repairs and Maintenance 11500—

Ⓔ From discussions with Carl Hayes, this appears to be a major renovation of Store 2. Potentially should be charged to "Leasehold Improvements". Further investigation is needed to determine Outlook.

* Auditor's note: In practice the details of these payments would be given. We have shortened them because of space limitations.

Exhibit 9-5

Lakeside Company

GENERAL LEDGER - ACCOUNT NUMBER 111-1
BUILDING - WAREHOUSE/OFFICE

REFERENCE	DEBIT	CREDIT	BALANCE
Balance - January 1, 1994			$163,500
Invoice # 3145	21,800		185,300
Invoice #3189	16,900		202,200
Invoice #3214	25,300		227,500
Invoice #3228	14,600		242,100
Totals	78,600		
Balance			$242,100

Exhibit 9-6

INVOICES

Livingstone Grading and Contracting
Box 911
Staples Mill Road
Richmond, VA 23220

To: Lakeside Company
　　Box 887, Richmond, VA 23173
　　　　October 5, 1994

For Services Rendered:

Grading of Land and
Pouring of Foundation
for New Warehouse

Total Amount Due　　　　　$21,800.00

This Bill Is Due Immediately

> **Lakeside**
> Invoice # 3145
> Date Received: 10/7/94
> Check # 2481
> Debit 111-1
> Approval *Rogers*

HEILMAN CONSTRUCTION
8737 Patterson Ave.　Richmond, VA 23229
Telephone: 272-4491

All Work is Done on Net 30 Terms

Contract for:　The Lakeside Company
　　　　　　　　Box 887
　　　　　　　　Richmond, VA 23173

First Installment on Construction of New Warehouse.

This Installment Represents Work for Month of October

　　　　Amount Due - $16,900

> **Lakeside**
> Invoice # 3189
> Date Received: 11/6/94
> Check # 2541
> Debit 111-1
> Approval *Rogers*

Exhibit 9-6 (continued)

HEILMAN CONSTRUCTION 8737 Patterson Ave. Richmond, VA 23229 Telephone: 272-4491 All Work is Done on Net 30 Terms	*"Roofing Repairs and Construction"* **Haymes Roofing** 11619 Huguenot Road Richmond, VA 23234 Phone: 285-6295 or 274-6119

Contract for: The Lakeside Company
                 Box 887
                 Richmond, VA 23173
	Lakeside Company
	Box 887
	Richmond, VA 23173

Heilman Construction:

Second Installment on Construction of New Warehouse.

This Installment Represents Work for Month of November

Amount Due - $25,300

Lakeside
Invoice # 3214
Date Received: 12/9/94
Check # 2622
Debit 111-1
Approval *Rogers*

Haymes Roofing:

Roofing Repair and Construction on New Warehouse

Repair	$ 3,500
New Addition	11,100
Total Bill	$21,800

Work performed 11/15/94 thru 12/10/94

Lakeside
Invoice # 3228
Date Received: 12/15/94
Check # 2668
Debit 111-1
Approval *Rogers*

Exhibit 9-6 (continued)

HEILMAN CONSTRUCTION 8737 Patterson Ave. Richmond, VA 23229 Telephone: 272-4491 All Work is Done on Net 30 Terms	**Gaines Electrical Company** *"Serving Richmond Since 1957"*

Contract for: The Lakeside Company
                          Box 887
                          Richmond, VA 23173
 	
First Installment on Construction of New Warehouse.
 	
This Installment Represents Work for Month of December
 	
Amount Due - $17,100
	Richmond, Virginia
	
	Lakeside Company
	Box 887
	Richmond, Virginia 23173
	
	Ellectrical service on new construction
	for two weeks -- 12/28/94 - 1/8/95
	
	                              $4,800.00
	
	Terms: Net 30

Lakeside
Invoice # 3316
Date Received: 1/7/95
Check # 2780
Debit 111-1
Approval Roger
	Mail Checks to: Gaines Electrical Company
	                              Box 9166, Broad Street
	                              Richmond. VA 23219

	Lakeside Invoice # 3408 Date Received: 1/15/95 Check # 2881 Debit 111-1 Approval Roger

(The Gaines Electrical Company header is circled.)

CASE 10

REVIEW OF SUBSEQUENT EVENTS

During the last part of January, 1995, Carole Mitchell, senior auditor for the CPA firm of Abernethy and Chapman, was in the process of finishing the substantive testing for the Lakeside Company audit engagement. She hoped to complete field work by February 9 in order to have the final audit report delivered to the client by the February 22 deadline.

The examination had moved into its final phases and Mitchell, along with the other members of the audit team, were now accumulating evidence relating to the weeks subsequent to the end of the client's fiscal year. They had already performed the following testing procedures in the period since December 31, 1994:

1. Confirmations were returned to the auditors by each of the banks that dealt with Lakeside during the year. These documents disclosed year-end balances and the terms for all accounts and loans. The confirmations also requested the banks to furnish information on certain types of contingent liabilities such as discounted notes receivable. Upon receipt of each confirmation, Paul Rubens reconciled the reported balances to Lakeside's December 31, 1994 records to ensure their agreement. In addition, Carole Mitchell verified that the terms of each loan were consistent with the accounting records of the company. She also made certain that all loans were being appropriately disclosed within the financial statements.

2. Cut-off statements were received from each bank for all of Lakeside's checking accounts. These statements covered the period from January 1, 1995, through January 10, 1995. Rubens verified that all cancelled checks and deposits returned by the bank agreed with the year-end reconciliations prepared by Lakeside employees.

3. Another Abernethy and Chapman auditor, Art Heyman, established the validity of the year-end inventory and sales cut-off. Using the bills of lading prepared between December 28, 1994, and January 2, 1995, (see Exhibit 8-3), Heyman located the corresponding sales invoices to determine the appropriate date for recognizing each sale. This information was then compared with the actual recording of the transaction in Lakeside's Sales Journal. Heyman also traced the receiving reports for the same period to the purchase invoices to ascertain the date on which title changed hands for each incoming shipment. These dates were then reconciled to the Inventory Purchases Journal to ensure that all purchases were recorded in the correct time period.

4. Wallace Andrews, the audit manager for the Lakeside engagement, read the minutes of a board of directors meeting held on January 17, 1995. The directors had met primarily to discuss two matters: the expansion of the warehouse facility and damage to Store 2 caused by an electrical fire on January 5, 1995. At this meeting, Rogers stated that the construction was progressing as expected and should be completed during March at a cost of approximately $220,000. He also reported that an electrical malfunction in Store 2 had started a small fire on the evening of January 5. Actual fire damage was limited but water and heavy smoke had caused over $40,000 in inventory losses. Rogers indicated that the company's insurance would cover between 60% and 80% of this amount. As a final action, the board of directors declared a cash dividend of $8,000 to be paid to shareholders on January 31, 1995.

5. Carole Mitchell began to review a portion of the invoices received by Lakeside during the month of January, 1995. She also intended to analyze the company's cash disbursements for this same period. Both procedures were designed to detect any liabilities that were unrecorded by the client as of December 31, 1994.

6. Mitchell performed an extensive search for contingent losses. She talked with Lakeside's management about the possible existence of such losses, read correspondence as well as invoices received from the law firm of Benzinger and Dawkins (the outside legal counsel employed by Lakeside), and reviewed all bank confirmations along with the company's current contracts. None of these procedures indicated the presence of any type of contingent loss as of December 31, 1994. A letter was then mailed to Benzinger and Dawkins stating that the management of Lakeside did not believe any material contingencies existed. On February 2, 1995, Abernethy and Chapman received a response stating that the law firm did not differ with the evaluation of contingencies made by the Lakeside management.

7. A related parties inquiry letter was sent to the Rogers Development Company owned by Mr. and Mrs. Rogers. This letter asked about the extent and nature of dealings with Lakeside, as well as all amounts due to or from that company. Rogers' reply described the lease agreement on Store 7, but nothing more.

8. A final analytical review was performed by Mitchell. This review is in addition to the one done during the preliminary stages of the audit (see Case 3). The purpose of the earlier analytical review was to help identify critical areas for further substantive testing. The purpose of this final analytical review is to ensure that nothing unusual has occurred during the latter stages of the audit. If unusual fluctuations occur, then the auditor must investigate further.

One issue still concerned Mitchell. She had recently reviewed the year-end adjustment entries prepared by Lakeside. Most of these entries were quite routine: depreciation expense, payroll liability, interest expense accrual, etc. One entry though did catch her attention: a debit to Other Miscellaneous Expenses and a credit to Accrued Product Warranty for $45,465. When questioned, Mark Hayes, the controller, stated that this adjusting entry was made annually to recognize the company's obligation for future repairs on products that had been sold under warranty during the past year. He indicated that the former auditors, King and Associates, had suggested some years ago that Lakeside accrue .7% of its annual sales for this product warranty. Since that time, a similar adjusting entry had been made each year. Hayes stated that 1994 sales of $6,495,000 required an accrual of $45,465 based on the .7% rate.

In further discussion with Hayes, Mitchell discovered that Lakeside offers a six-month warranty on all merchandise. If any item malfunctions within that time, Lakeside will repair it at no cost to the customer. The services of several local repair shops are used for this purpose. When asked about the cost, Hayes responded, "It usually runs about $4,000 per month. The Cypress products are good; repairs are not that common."

Mitchell immediately went to Dan Cline, the audit partner on the engagement, for guidance. Estimating the potential liability of a six-month product warranty on $6.5 million in sales was an obvious audit concern. Cline agreed that additional evidence was needed to corroborate the accrued liability balance reported at December 31, 1994. He asked Mitchell to prepare a two-year history of repairs so that a determination could be made of the client's potential liability. Mitchell requested this data from Hayes and received the following:

MONTH 1993	SALES FOR MONTH	REPAIR EXPENSE FOR MONTH
January	$532,000	$3,013
February	316,000	3,018
March	359,000	4,691
April	479,000	4,439
May	486,000	3,005
June	414,000	3,049
July	371,000	2,866
August	460,000	2,866
September	442,000	4,116
October	533,000	3,804
November	586,000	3,542
December	800,000	3,730

MONTH 1994	SALES FOR MONTH	REPAIR EXPENSE FOR MONTH
January	$610,500	$4,313
February	381,000	4,750
March	346,000	3,973
April	557,000	4,439
May	590,000	4,818
June	409,000	4,449
July	422,000	4,075
August	550,000	3,542
September	511,000	4,181
October	602,500	5,206
November	642,000	4,830
December	874,000	4,741

In addition to the data presented above, Hayes was able to break down the repair expense for each month by the age of the item being repaired. This information is contained in Exhibit 10-1.

DISCUSSION QUESTIONS

(1) In examining a bank cut-off statement, what evidence is the auditor seeking?

(2) Why do auditors continue to send confirmation letters to banks if the client's account has been closed?

(3) The minutes of the board of directors meeting mentions three events that occurred in 1995: the continuing construction of the warehouse, the fire damage, and the declaration of a cash dividend. How would each affect the 1994 financial statements?

(4) What is the purpose of a cut-off test? Is the cut-off testing of inventory and sales of significant importance in the Lakeside engagement?

(5) Mitchell reviewed invoices and cash disbursements in search of any unrecorded liabilities. Why are unrecorded liabilities a special problem for an independent auditor?

(6) Why would the search for contingent losses be a major concern to an auditor?

(7) What information is included on a letter of confirmation mailed to the client's law firm?

(8) Abernethy and Chapman received a letter from the law firm of Benzinger and Dawkins indicating no differences with Lakeside's assessment of contingent losses. Assume that several days later the law firm resigned from any further association with Lakeside. What might this action indicate to the auditing firm and what steps should then be taken?

(9) The case states that a related parties inquiry letter was sent to the Rogers Development Company. What is the purpose of this document?

(10) According to Statement of Auditing Standard Number 57, "Auditing Accounting Estimates," the management of a reporting company must identify the relevant factors that may affect an accounting estimation and then accumulate relevant, sufficient, and reliable information on which to base the estimation. In estimating product warranty liability for 1994, what factors would possibly influence the management's judgment? What information should then be used by management in order to arrive at this estimation?

(11) According to Statement on Auditing Standard Number 57, "Auditing Accounting Estimates," auditors should develop their own independent expectation of an estimate to corroborate the reasonableness of any estimation made by management. For Lakeside's product warranty liability, how should the Abernethy and Chapman auditors go about deriving an independent expectation of the amount?

WRITTEN QUESTIONS

(1) Assume that Carole Mitchell has asked you to use the data presented in this case to compute an independent estimation of the accrued product warranty liability as of December 31, 1994. Since this figure will be an estimate, she wants you to prepare a work paper to indicate exactly how the estimation was derived. (DISK: CASE10.WKS)

LIBRARY ASSIGNMENT

(1) Read the following and other published information concerning the communication between the auditor and the client's lawyers:

"Communications Between Auditors and Lawyers for the Identification and Evaluation of Litigation, Claims, and Assessments," Accounting Horizons, June, 1989, p. 76.

"SAS No. 12: Inquiry of a Client's Lawyer Concerning Litigation, Claims, and Assessments," AICPA, 1976.

"Statement of Policy Regarding Lawyers' Responses to Auditors' Requests for Information," Business Lawyer, April, 1976, p. 1709.

"Attorney Responses to Audit Letters: The Problem of Disclosing Loss Contingencies Arising from Litigation and Unasserted Claims," New York University Law Review, November, 1976, p. 877.

"Auditing Litigation, Claims and Assessments," CPA Journal, April, 1988, p. 86.

One of the procedures Abernethy and Chapman did in this case is mail a letter to Lakeside's attorneys concerning litigation, claims and assessments. Write a report concerning the communication between the auditor and the client's lawyers. What items are communicated? Why is this communication necessary? What is the quality of these types of communications in terms of audit evidence?

Exhibit 10-1

Lakeside Company

SUMMARY OF PRODUCT WARRANTY EXPENSE (Prepared by Client)
January, 1993 through December, 1993

MONTH	January 1993	February 1993	March 1993	April 1993
Sales for Month	$532,000	$316,000	$359,000	$479,000
Returns During Month: From				
- Current Month Sales	$ 193	$ 137	$ 177	$ 222
- 1 Month Old Sales	445	533	388	329
- 2 Month Old Sales	599	693	837	319
- 3 Month Old Sales	555	423	1,287	875
- 4 Month Old Sales	570	658	986	1,188
- 5 Month Old Sales	328	289	763	1,021
- 6 Month Old Sales	323	285	253	485
Total	$ 3,013	$ 3,018	$ 4,691	$ 4,439

MONTH	May 1993	June 1993	July 1993	August 1993
Sales for Month	$486,000	$414,000	$371,000	$460,000
Returns During Month: From				
- Current Month Sales	$ 147	$ 61	$ 256	$ 284
- 1 Month Old Sales	369	514	276	313
- 2 Month Old Sales	481	480	625	429
- 3 Month Old Sales	662	658	591	441
- 4 Month Old Sales	343	320	456	702
- 5 Month Old Sales	792	571	205	228
- 6 Month Old Sales	211	445	457	251
Total	$ 3,005	$ 3,049	$ 2,866	$ 2,648

MONTH	September 1993	October 1993	November 1993	December 1993
Sales for Month	$442,000	$533,000	$586,000	$800,000
Returns During Month: From				
- Current Month Sales	$ 210	$ 292	$ 469	$ 505
- 1 Month Old Sales	497	559	583	563
- 2 Month Old Sales	569	462	629	666
- 3 Month Old Sales	797	541	639	664
- 4 Month Old Sales	1,029	735	512	604
- 5 Month Old Sales	812	698	490	456
- 6 Month Old Sales	202	517	220	272
Total	$ 4,116	$ 3,804	$ 3,542	$ 3,730

Exhibit 10-1 (Continued)

Lakeside Company

SUMMARY OF PRODUCT WARRANTY EXPENSE (Prepared by Client)
January, 1994 Through December, 1994

MONTH	January 1994	February 1994	March 1994	April 1994
Sales for Month	$610,500	$381,000	$346,000	$557,000
Returns During Month: From				
- Current Month Sales	$ 323	$ 336	$ 234	$ 335
- 1 Month Old Sales	948	969	366	351
- 2 Month Old Sales	657	885	861	397
- 3 Month Old Sales	917	845	1,074	915
- 4 Month Old Sales	594	625	798	1,201
- 5 Month Old Sales	675	699	500	657
- 6 Month Old Sales	199	391	140	583
Total	$ 4,313	$ 4,750	$ 3,973	$ 4,439

MONTH	May 1994	June 1994	July 1994	August 1994
Sales for Month	$590,000	$409,000	$422,000	$550,000
Returns During Month: From				
- Current Month Sales	$ 421	$ 368	$ 599	$ 251
- 1 Month Old Sales	670	736	442	337
- 2 Month Old Sales	410	766	684	516
- 3 Month Old Sales	580	527	1,054	947
- 4 Month Old Sales	1,023	549	292	718
- 5 Month Old Sales	1,010	808	519	468
- 6 Month Old Sales	704	695	485	305
Total	$ 4,818	$ 4,449	$ 4,075	$ 3,542

MONTH	September 1994	October 1994	November 1994	December 1994
Sales for Month	$511,000	$602,500	$642,000	$874,000
Returns During Month: From				
- Current Month Sales	$ 277	$ 220	$ 423	$ 504
- 1 Month Old Sales	752	738	769	785
- 2 Month Old Sales	375	1,203	830	934
- 3 Month Old Sales	664	749	852	876
- 4 Month Old Sales	894	627	824	602
- 5 Month Old Sales	575	999	553	524
- 6 Month Old Sales	644	670	579	516
Total	$ 4,181	$ 5,206	$ 4,830	$ 4,741

CASE 11

SAMPLING FOR ATTRIBUTES

On February 4, 1995, Jan Luck, Assistant Controller for the Lakeside Company, delivered to the Abernethy and Chapman auditors an analysis of all invoices received by the company during December and January. A total of 283 invoices had been located by Luck with assistance from the independent auditors. These bills represented a variety of charges incurred by each of the company's seven stores including rent, heating oil, electricity, insurance, water, maintenance fees, property taxes, and advertising. In addition, a number of the invoices reflected the travel and lodging expenses of the members of Lakeside's sales staff.

For each of these invoices, Luck had scheduled the total amount owed by Lakeside, the expense or asset account to be charged, the due date, and the date paid or the date on which payment would be made. Luck also calculated and listed the portion of each bill that was legally owed by Lakeside as of December 31, 1994. Based on this analysis, accrued expenses totaling $46,311 were to be recorded by the company as a year-end adjusting entry.

Carole Mitchell, senior auditor with the Abernethy and Chapman organization, was aware that she would have to verify the accuracy of the $46,311 accrual. As with all client prepared computations, the auditing firm had a responsibility to establish the validity of this liability. In this instance, though, the need to review the analysis was especially important since a large change was being made in the net income figure reported by the client.

Mitchell was primarily interested in Luck's ability to allocate these expenses correctly between 1994 and 1995. In arriving at the $46,311 accrual, every invoice had been examined by Luck in order to assign the appropriate amount to each period. Because of the potential audit time involved, Mitchell wanted to avoid having to assign a member of her staff to review and check all 283 documents. Instead, she hoped to validate the client's work by analyzing a representative sample of these invoices. Since Mitchell was concerned with the occurrence of errors in the allocation process, she decided to apply statistical sampling for attributes, a testing technique frequently utilized by the Abernethy and Chapman auditors.

Based on Mitchell's previous work with sampling for attributes, she realized that she had to establish three parameters corresponding to her judgment of the client and the importance of the procedure being evaluated:

<u>Acceptable Risk of Overreliance (ARO)</u>. Because of the decision to sample, Mitchell understood that a degree of risk was involved. Since all of the invoices were not to be reviewed, a possibility existed that the auditing firm would evaluate Luck's work as being reliable when, in fact, it was not. After some consideration, Mitchell chose a 10% risk of overreliance for this test. She was willing to accept the statistical fact that one time in 10 the sample would mislead her into relying on work that was not actually acceptable.

<u>Estimated Population Exception Rate (EPER)</u>. Based on the degree of complexity involved in the allocation process, Mitchell realized that Luck would probably commit some errors; perfection was not anticipated for this type of task. In a statistical sampling plan designed to determine the frequency of an attribute, the auditor must estimate an actual occurrence rate. From discussions with Luck as well as observations of her work, Mitchell believed that a 3% exception rate should be considered normal.

<u>Tolerable Exception Rate (TER)</u>. Finally, Mitchell had to address the possibility that the errors existing in the population were of a quantity significant enough to nullify reliance on Luck's work. Mitchell decided that if a sample indicated the presence of an error rate in excess of 6% she would be forced to devise alternative procedures to verify the end-of-year accrual.

Mitchell's next concern was the determination of the number of invoices that had to be selected to furnish the desired level of assurance. Because of the frequent use of sampling for attributes, Abernethy and Chapman provides its auditors with statistical tables to assist them in the implementation of this testing procedure. Based on predetermined mathematical calculations, the proper size for any sample can be found on these tables. The specific table to be used is determined by the auditor's decision concerning the acceptable risk of overreliance. Exhibit 11-1 presents the table for a 10% ARO, the level chosen by Mitchell for this test. The appropriate sample size is a function of the EPER (left column) and the chosen TER (top row).

After Mitchell selects the sample and analyzes individual items, conclusions about the population as a whole will be derived by using a second table. Exhibit 11-2 presents mathematical results based on the auditor's desire to limit risk of overreliance to 10%. The sample size (left column) and the actual number of exceptions discovered in the sample (top row) provide the computed upper exception rate (CUER) anticipated in the population. However, this upper exception rate is not intended as a precise indication of the percentage of mistakes that are present. Rather, Mitchell can assume, given the three parameters that she has set, that the exception rate in the 283 allocations is no higher than the percentage indicated in Exhibit 11-2. Consequently, if the computed upper exception rate is equal to or less than the 6%

tolerable exception rate established as a prerequisite, the number of errors in Luck's work will be judged as acceptable. Mitchell will still have to analyze the individual errors found in the sample since both the type as well as quantity of mistakes must be evaluated.

Prior to the start of this testing, Mitchell makes one final calculation. The table produced in Exhibit 11-1 is based on a large population and a sampling plan with replacement where items chosen will be recorded and then returned to the population. Lakeside has only 283 invoices and the auditors will not replace selected items to avoid having them chosen a second time. Mitchell is aware that a finite correction factor can be applied to adjust the information found in this table so that it corresponds with the client's population. In some cases, this adjustment significantly reduces the required number of items to be tested, thus, increasing audit efficiency. The formula applied for this purpose is

$$\text{Appropriate Sample Size} = n'/(1 + n'/N)$$

where: n' = sample size found in table

N = number of items in the population.

DISCUSSION QUESTIONS

(1) Independent auditors must evaluate an entire set of financial statements. Considering that risk is always involved in selecting only a sample, why are auditors willing to accept less than a complete review and analysis when accumulating evidence?

(2) Incorporating statistics into a sampling plan creates additional work and complexity for the auditor. What are the advantages of sampling plans that are based on statistical laws and guidelines?

(3) Sampling for attributes is a procedure that is frequently associated in auditing with the tests of controls. Why is this type of statistical sampling especially important in evaluating the degree to which a client's internal control procedures are effective?

(4) When applying sampling for attributes, auditors often attempt to measure several attributes within a single testing plan. What is the reason for this approach? What other attribute could be tested by Mitchell in this case?

(5) Mitchell has indicated that she assumes Luck has made some mistakes in allocating year-end expenses. How can the auditor tolerate using work that is known to be incorrect? Why might an individual such as Luck commit errors in arriving at a year-end adjustment?

(6) Mitchell anticipates that Luck has committed errors in 3% (EPER) of the allocations made. How does an auditor arrive at this type of estimation?

(7) Mitchell has decided that Luck's work will be viewed as being reliable if the sample indicates 6% (TER) or fewer errors. What factors should have influenced the auditor's selection of this parameter?

(8) Assume that Mitchell's computations indicate an appropriate sample size of 40. She selects this number of invoices and reviews the accuracy of Luck's allocations. Mitchell discovers two errors. What conclusion will she reach based on the parameters established?

(9) Assume that Mitchell selects a sample of 40 items and determines from these allocations that Luck's work is not reliable. What alternatives are available to the auditor?

WRITTEN QUESTION

(1) To ensure adequate documentation, the CPA firm of Abernethy and Chapman requires its auditors to complete a preprinted form whenever sampling for attributes is being applied. This document is presented in Exhibit 11-3. Complete the form using the data provided in this case. Assume that a sample of the appropriate size is drawn by Mitchell using a random number generator on her computer. Two errors are discovered in the sample although both are of relatively small amounts and appear to be caused by addition errors.
(DISK: CASE11.DOC)

LIBRARY ASSIGNMENT

(1) Read the following, as well as other published materials concerning audit sampling:

"Statistical Sampling in Public Accounting," CPA Journal, July, 1980, p. 20.
"Statistical Sampling vs. Judgmental Sampling: An Empirical Study of Auditing the Accounts Receivable of a Small Retail Store," Accounting Review, January, 1971, p. 119.
"AICPA Nonstatistical Audit Sampling Guidelines: A Simulation," Auditing: A Journal of Practice and Theory, Fall, 1991, p. 33.
"Audit Sampling--Dealing with the Problems," Journal of Accountancy, December, 1988, p. 58.

Write a report discussing the use of sampling in conducting an audit. To what extent should auditors use sampling? Is statistical sampling better than judgmental sampling? What problems do auditors face when using sampling methods?

Exhibit 11-1
DETERMINING SAMPLE SIZE FOR ATTRIBUTES SAMPLING
10 Percent Risk of Overreliance

Expected Population Exception Rate (in %)	\multicolumn{11}{c}{Tolerable Exception Rate (in %)}
	2	3	4	5	6	7	8	9	10	15	20
0.00	114	76	57	45	38	32	28	25	22	15	11
0.25	194	129	96	77	64	55	48	42	38	25	18
0.50	194	129	96	77	64	55	48	42	38	25	18
1.00	*	176	96	77	64	55	48	42	38	25	18
1.25	*	221	132	77	64	55	48	42	38	25	18
1.50	*	*	132	105	64	55	48	42	38	25	18
2.00	*	*	198	132	88	75	48	42	38	25	18
2.25	*	*	*	132	88	75	65	42	38	25	18
2.50	*	*	*	158	110	75	65	58	38	25	18
3.00	*	*	*	*	132	94	65	58	52	25	18
3.25	*	*	*	*	153	113	82	58	52	25	18
3.50	*	*	*	*	194	113	82	73	52	25	18
4.00	*	*	*	*	*	149	98	73	65	25	18
4.50	*	*	*	*	*	218	130	87	65	34	18
5.00	*	*	*	*	*	*	160	115	78	34	18
5.50	*	*	*	*	*	*	*	142	103	34	18

* Sample is too large to be cost-effective for most audit applications.

Exhibit 11-2
EVALUATING SAMPLE RESULTS USING
ATTRIBUTES SAMPLING
10 Percent Risk of Overreliance

Sample Size	\multicolumn{11}{c}{Actual Number of Exceptions Found}
	0	1	2	3	4	5	6	7	8	9	10
20	10.9	18.1	*	*	*	*	*	*	*	*	*
25	8.8	14.7	19.9	*	*	*	*	*	*	*	*
30	7.4	12.4	16.8	*	*	*	*	*	*	*	*
35	6.4	10.7	14.5	18.1	*	*	*	*	*	*	*
40	5.6	9.4	12.8	15.9	19.0	*	*	*	*	*	*
45	5.0	8.4	11.4	14.2	17.0	19.6	*	*	*	*	*
50	4.5	7.6	10.3	12.9	15.4	17.8	*	*	*	*	*
55	4.1	6.9	9.4	11.7	14.0	16.2	18.4	*	*	*	*
60	3.8	6.3	8.6	10.8	12.9	14.9	16.9	18.8	*	*	*
70	3.2	5.4	7.4	9.3	11.1	12.8	14.6	16.2	17.9	19.5	*
80	2.8	4.8	6.5	8.3	9.7	11.3	12.8	14.3	15.7	17.2	18.6
90	2.5	4.3	5.8	7.3	8.7	10.1	11.4	12.7	14.0	15.3	16.6
100	2.3	3.8	5.2	6.6	7.8	9.1	10.3	11.5	12.7	13.8	15.0
120	1.9	3.2	4.4	5.5	6.6	7.6	8.6	9.6	10.6	11.6	12.5
160	1.4	2.4	3.3	4.1	4.9	5.7	6.5	7.2	8.0	8.7	9.5
200	1.1	1.9	2.6	3.3	4.0	4.6	5.2	5.8	6.4	7.0	7.6

* Over 20 percent

Exhibit 11-3

Abernethy and Chapman

SAMPLING FOR ATTRIBUTES

Client: _____

Year Ending: _____

Audit Area: _____

Date of Testing: _____

(1) - State the objectives of the audit testing:

(2) - Define the attribute or attributes to be estimated:

(3) - Define the population:

(4) - Define the sampling unit:

(5) - Specify the acceptable risk of overreliance and discuss any factors affecting this decision:

(6) - Estimate the exception rate of the population and discuss any factors affecting this estimation:

(7) - Specify the tolerable exception rate and discuss any factors affecting this decision:

(8) - Indicate the sample size and show the use of the finite correction factor if applicable:

(9) - Indicate the method used to draw a random sample:

(10) - Indicate the number of exceptions discovered, the rate of exceptions in the sample, and the computed upper exception rate in the population:

(11) - From a quantitative perspective, is the population reliable (include the rationale for your answer):

(12) - Describe the types of exceptions that were found:

(13) - Recommendations:

CASE 12

SAMPLING FOR VARIABLES - DIFFERENCE ESTIMATION

Note: The material presented herein is based on the problem introduced in Case 11. Once again, the auditor is attempting to obtain assurance as to the validity of the client's representation. However, in this current case, an alternative approach is being examined. Although the previous case should serve as background information, the assumption is made here in Case 12 that a sampling for attributes plan has not been applied.

During the later stages of every Abernethy and Chapman engagement, the partner in charge performs a comprehensive review of all work papers created by the audit team. Although each of these documents is examined for completeness, clarity, and understandability, the primary purpose of this procedure is to ensure that sufficient, competent evidence has been accumulated to substantiate the audit opinion. To stress the importance of this responsibility, the firm requires the partner to "sign-off" on each major audit area to indicate the belief that reasonable assurance has been achieved that no material misstatements exist within the client's financial statements.

Dan Cline is the partner in charge of the 1994 audit of the Lakeside Company. During his final review on every engagement, Cline creates a list of issues that he believes need to be clarified or resolved before the audit is concluded. One of the areas that Cline has noted in the Lakeside examination is the cut-off testing performed on the client's year-end expense accrual. An adjustment to record a $46,311 liability was proposed by Lakeside and tentatively accepted by Carole Mitchell, the audit senior. According to her work papers, Mitchell analyzed 30 out of 283 invoices prior to recommending that this accrual be accepted. Cline was concerned to note that the liability computed on 4 of these 30 invoices contained errors committed by Lakeside personnel. Only about 10% of the invoices had been reviewed by Mitchell and those documents reflected a 13.3% error rate. Cline was not satisfied that sufficient corroborating evidence had been obtained to substantiate the $46,311 accrual.

In a subsequent discussion to finalize any remaining audit actions, Mitchell and Cline assessed the need for additional evidence to validate the client's expense accrual:

MITCHELL: I judgmentally chose a sample size of 30 invoices. I believed then, as I do now, that I could arrive at a proper conclusion about the total accrual by examining approximately 10% of the invoices. Mistakes were found, which I have documented, but they involved relatively small amounts and did not show any suspicious trends. I recognize that $46,311 is not a precisely correct amount, but I still believe that this accrual is a fairly presented figure. I see no reason to waste further audit time.

CLINE: I don't necessarily disagree that Lakeside's balance is fairly presented; I just don't believe we have proven that assertion in our work papers. If the entire population contains 13.3% errors, approximately 38 of the 283 accruals are incorrect. That represents a lot of mistakes and we have not computed a possible total dollar amount for these errors. Even small errors can add up to a large deviation if enough are present. Furthermore, the population may actually hold more than 13.3% errors. Our single sample of only 30 invoices might not have been representative.

MITCHELL: In that case, I see no alternative but to examine more of the invoices.

CLINE: That approach would indeed provide us with a better estimation of the error rate. However, we already know the population has errors. I am more interested in the dollar impact of those mistakes. Do they net to zero or $20,000 or perhaps even more?

MITCHELL: We can always recompute an accrual for each of the invoices. The total amount of the liability could be determined to the penny in that way.

CLINE: Examining the entire population would take too long and we really have no need for that degree of accuracy. I will be satisfied if we can verify that Lakeside's $46,311 figure is within $8,000 of the real total. Could we use some form of sampling for variables plan and estimate the total dollar amount of these errors?

MITCHELL: I suppose so but I have had little experience in applying sampling for variables concepts.

CLINE: Why don't you talk with Mike Farrell? He is our partner specializing in statistical sampling. I am certain that he can assist you in designing a statistical sampling plan to determine the validity of the client's accrual. After you complete the testing, let's review the results to see if we have the assurance we need.

Mitchell did approach Farrell with her problem and he provided the following information:

"Several types of statistical sampling approaches exist but each is based on selecting a representative sample. A truly representative sample has the same characteristics as the population. Thus, evaluations and decisions can be made about the population just by looking at the sample. To achieve a reasonable degree of representation, two conditions must be met. First, a large enough sample is selected, and second, all items are chosen randomly. Mathematical equations are used to project the appropriate sample size while our firm generates random numbers with a computer program.

"Sampling for variables is a technique used specifically for calculating a total which in this case is the client's expense accrual. After you have defined the population and the sampling unit, an estimation is made of the standard deviation of the individual units within the population. Standard deviation is a statistical measure of the dispersion of items from their arithmetic mean. Are the individual numbers close together or far apart? This figure is important since a larger dispersion necessitates a larger sample being drawn. Auditors derive an estimation of the standard deviation by a mathematical formula. Several variations of this equation exist but at Abernethy and Chapman the following model is used:

$$\text{Estimated Standard Deviation} = \sqrt{\frac{[\Sigma(x^2) - n(y)^2]}{n-1}}$$

"In this formula, x is the value of each unit sampled while y is the average of these items. The letter 'n' represents the number of items selected. Although we usually need to choose between 30 and 50 items for this computation, five can be used here for demonstration purposes. Assume that the five numbers selected had values of $1, $5, $5, $7, and $12.

x	x^2
1	1
5	25
5	25
7	49
12	144
30	244

$y = 30/5$ or $\underline{6}$

"With this small sample, the standard deviation would be:

$$\sqrt{\frac{(244) - (5)(6)^2}{4}} = \sqrt{\frac{244 - 180}{4}} = \sqrt{16} = 4$$

"Once the standard deviation has been estimated, the auditor must establish the maximum level of risk that can be tolerated. In sampling for variables, two separate risks are encountered. First, an acceptable risk of incorrect acceptance, referred to as ARIA, has to be set. This percentage represents the possibility that Abernethy and Chapman will accept the client's $46,311 accrual even though, in actuality, the figure is materially in error. Setting a risk level for incorrect acceptance is a serious responsibility since it establishes the possibility that the auditor could render an unqualified opinion on statements that are not fairly presented. Fortunately, the risk of incorrect acceptance can be lessened by an effective control structure as well as any other substantive procedures the auditor is performing in the area.

"Auditors also have to set an acceptable level for the risk of incorrect rejection, commonly known as ARIR. In the Lakeside case, our firm faces the possibility of rejecting the $46,311 accrual based on a sample when the figure may in fact be fairly presented. Incorrect rejection usually causes the auditor to perform extra substantive tests that are not necessary. This causes inefficiencies. As a worse possibility, the firm might qualify financial statements that are actually fairly presented.

"Through the use of sampling for variables, the auditor is able to compute the correct sample size based on predetermined limits as to the risks being taken. An acceptable risk of incorrect acceptance is required as well as an acceptable risk of incorrect rejection. Both of these figures are ultimately derived from the auditor's judgment. Unfortunately, the two risk levels cannot be entered directly into the various statistical equations. Instead, equivalent confidence coefficients, sometimes referred to as Z values, are utilized for mathematical purposes. These equivalents can be found from a statistical table (see Exhibit 12-1).

"After estimating the standard deviation and setting the two acceptable risk levels, the next preliminary task is to establish a tolerable misstatement, the amount of mistake that the auditor is willing to accept in the client's reported balance. Apparently, from your discussion with Dan Cline, that figure will be $8,000 in this audit test of the accrual balance.

"Before proceeding to the statistical formulas, a decision is needed as to the specific type of sampling for variables plan to be applied. For example, one common approach is referred to as mean-per-unit sampling. Using this method, the arithmetic average of the sample is assumed to be the same as that of the population. As an illustration, if the average end-of-year accrual found in a Lakeside sample came to $165, that figure would be multiplied by the 283 invoices to arrive at an estimated total. Unfortunately, one major problem often hinders the usefulness of the mean-per-unit approach. The standard deviation of most populations is usually so high that a very large sample is necessary; thus, the principal benefit of sampling, saving time, is defeated.

"I would suggest that you consider using an alternative known as difference estimation. It is appropriate when individual book values can be compared with audited balances to arrive at a population of differences. This statistical sampling technique estimates the total of the differences rather than the total of the audited values. For Lakeside, the year-end expense accrual would not be calculated directly, but rather its distance from $46,311. Since the individual differences in most populations tend to be zero or small numbers, the standard deviation will be relatively low. Thus, a smaller sample is required to achieve the auditor's acceptable risk levels. The Lakeside situation lends itself to this procedure since the client already has an accrual for each invoice that can now be measured against an audited value.

"To begin using difference estimation, I would utilize the 30 items that have already been randomly selected (Exhibit 12-2) to compute an advance estimation of the standard deviation. The formula previously discussed should be used for this purpose. Remember though that the items being sampled are the differences. For example, if the client reports an accrual of $140 but our analysis indicates an actual expense of $145, a difference of +$5 exists. This +$5 figure is a unit within our population and will be used in calculating the standard deviation and then the total difference that the actual accrual is from $46,311. That is, use the "difference" column in Exhibit 12-2 to compute the standard deviation.

"After the standard deviation of the differences is estimated, the appropriate sample size can be calculated using the following formula:

$$\text{Sample Size} = \frac{(SD \times [Za + Zr] \times N)^2}{TM - E}$$

where:

    N   =   population size
    Za   =   confidence coefficient for the acceptable risk of incorrect acceptance (Exhibit 12-1)

Zr = confidence coefficient for the acceptable risk of incorrect rejection (Exhibit 12-1)
SD = estimate of the standard deviation of the differences
TM = tolerable misstatement of the population
E = point estimate of population misstatement

"We have discussed all of the elements of this equation except for E, the point estimate of the population misstatement. By looking at last year's audit or by examining the quality of the client's work, the total dollar misstatement existing within the population can be anticipated. Since our firm did not audit Lakeside last year, you may want to use the average misstatement in the initial sample of 30 invoices as the estimation of this figure.

"Once the sample size has been determined, the appropriate number of invoices should be selected randomly and examined. Any difference between the client accrual and the audited balance is listed. To save time, most auditors would include within their sample the 30 items previously analyzed in determining the standard deviation. The average difference for the entire sample is then computed with that amount being considered a reflection of the population of 283 items. For example, if the average difference of the sample proved to be +$10, we would estimate that the accrual actually exceeded $46,311 by $2,830 or +$10 multiplied by the 283 invoices.

"This $2,830 figure, however, is just a single point. Since only a portion of the population was examined, this degree of absolute accuracy is not possible. Hence, the auditor computes a range, a precision interval, that serves as the actual estimate of the population total. In deriving this precision interval, the auditor must first reestimate the standard deviation since a larger sample is now available. The standard deviation formula previously discussed is again used for this purpose with the refined figure helping to ensure the accuracy of the final evaluation.

"The precision interval can then be calculated using another mathematical equation:

$$\text{Precision Interval} = N \times Za \times \frac{SD}{\sqrt{n}} \times \frac{(N-n)}{\sqrt{N}}$$

where:

N = population size
n = total sample size
SD = estimate of standard deviation (second computation)
Za = confidence coefficient for the acceptable risk of incorrect acceptance (Exhibit 12-1)

"To illustrate, assume that the point estimation of the errors is calculated as being $2,830 above book value. According to the sample, the client's total appears to be understated by that amount. Assume also that a precision interval of $5,000 is computed using the above equation. Given the risk parameters that have been established by the auditor, the actual error apparently lies somewhere between an understatement of $7,830 ($2,830 + $5,000) and an overstatement of $2,170 ($2,830 - $5,000). Because sampling has been used, the exact population total cannot be specified within that range. However, since Cline wants assurance that the client figure is within $8,000 of the real total, the auditing firm can accept the $46,311 as fairly presented. No portion of the computed range falls outside of that $8,000 boundary; the risk is acceptable. Conversely, if the sample had indicated a range from an overstatement of $1,000 to an understatement of $9,000, the client's accrual could not be accepted without further testing; the interval achieved would not be completely within the $8,000 tolerable risk level. The $46,311 reported balance might still be fairly presented but too much risk would be involved in accepting the figure without gathering additional audit evidence."

After talking with Farrell, Carole Mitchell met again briefly with Cline to establish guidelines for this testing. The decision was made that a tolerable error of $8,000 should be used. In addition, an acceptable risk of incorrect acceptance of 10% was set along with a 30% level for the risk of incorrect rejection.

DISCUSSION QUESTIONS

(1) Carole Mitchell attempted to use judgmental sampling to verify the client's accrual in this case while Dan Cline opted for statistical sampling. What are the advantages and disadvantages of each approach?

(2) Exhibit 12-2 presents the results of Mitchell's initial testing. Was Cline correct in seeking additional audit evidence?

(3) Statistical sampling is occasionally criticized for preventing the auditor from introducing personal judgment into a particular test. Is this assertion valid?

(4) Statistical sampling has also been criticized for being a slow, time-consuming process relative to judgmental sampling. Is this assertion valid?

(5) An auditor may utilize sampling for attributes in some tests and sampling for variables in others. How is the decision made as to which of these methods should be applied?

(6) Assume that Mitchell conducts her sampling plan and calculates the estimation of the total deviations to be +$3,760 with a precision interval of $5,200. What will be her conclusion about the population and what actions should be taken next by the auditors?

WRITTEN QUESTIONS

(1) To ensure adequate documentation, the CPA firm of Abernethy and Chapman requires its auditors to complete preprinted forms whenever sampling for variables is being applied.

 (A) Exhibit 12-4 presents the document to be used in computing a representative sample size. Complete this form using the data provided in this case. (DISK:CASE12.DOC)

 (B) Exhibit 12-5 presents the document to be used in evaluating the results of a difference estimation sample. Assume that Mitchell has computed the need for a sample size of 50 invoices.* Consequently, she selects the additional items found in Exhibit 12-3 using a computer generated list of random numbers. Complete the form found in Exhibit 12-5 based on the data provided in this case. (DISK: CASE12.DOC)

*Note: Sample sizes used in actual difference estimation plans might be larger than indicated here. Sample sizes have been kept small in order to be more manageable.

(2) Prepare the auditor's report that you believe is warranted for the Lakeside Company's 1994 financial statements based on the information contained in the first 12 cases. Assume that any facts not explicitly covered in these cases would not influence the decision as to the type of opinion to be rendered.

Exhibit 12-1

CONFIDENCE COEFFICIENTS
ACCEPTABLE LEVELS OF RISK

Acceptable Risk of Incorrect Acceptance (ARIA)	Acceptable Risk of Incorrect Rejection (ARIR)	Confidence Coefficient (Z Value)
2.5%	5.0%	1.96
5.0%	10.0%	1.64
10.0%	20.0%	1.28
12.5%	25.0%	1.15
15.0%	30.0%	1.04
20.0%	40.0%	.84
25.0%	50.0%	.67
30.0%	60.0%	.52
40.0%	80.0%	.25
50.0%	100.0%	.00

Exhibit 12-2

INITIAL SAMPLE OF YEAR-END INVOICES

Invoice	Book Value*	Audited Value*	Difference
1	$1,347	$1,347	-0-
2	44	44	-0-
3	168	168	-0-
4	-0-**	-0-	-0-
5	135	340	$ 205
6	-0-	-0-	-0-
7	802	802	-0-
8	76	76	-0-
9	126	126	-0-
10	-0-	-0-	-0-
11	269	269	-0-
12	488	488	-0-
13	561	561	-0-
14	-0-	49	49
15	102	102	-0-
16	22	22	-0-
17	410	300	(110)
18	-0-	-0-	-0-
19	176	176	-0-
20	88	88	-0-
21	400	400	-0-
22	247	247	-0-
23	120	276	156
24	55	55	-0-
25	131	131	-0-
26	1,088	1,088	-0-
27	-0-	-0-	-0-
28	-0-	-0-	-0-
29	50	50	-0-
30	632	632	-0-

*Rounded

**Zero balances represent invoices received in January that were entirely for January expenses.

Exhibit 12-3

ADDITIONAL SAMPLE OF 20 INVOICES

Invoice	Book Value*	Audited Value*	Difference
31	$ 331	$ 331	-0-
32	-0-	-0-	-0-
33	211	211	-0-
34	75	75	-0-
35	108	108	-0-
36	549	549	-0-
37	35	35	-0-
38	297	200	$ (97)
39	380	380	-0-
40	50	50	-0-
41	-0-	-0-	-0-
42	185	185	-0-
43	400	400	-0-
44	124	124	-0-
45	250	100	(150)
46	24	24	-0-
47	-0-	47	47
48	278	278	-0-
49	-0-	-0-	-0-
50	-0-	-0-	-0-

*Rounded

Exhibit 12-4

Abernethy and Chapman

**DETERMINATION OF SAMPLE SIZE
SAMPLING FOR VARIABLES**

Client: _____

Form Completed By: _____

Audit Area: _____

Date of Testing: _____ Year Ending: _____

(1) Estimate the standard deviation of the population. Show the formula being used and identify each element within this formula.

(2) Specify the acceptable level of risk for incorrect acceptance. Identify the confidence coefficient (Z value) for this percentage. Include any considerations that were used in arriving at this parameter.

(3) Specify the acceptable level of risk for incorrect rejection. Identify the confidence coefficient (Z value) for this percentage. Include any considerations that were used in arriving at this parameter.

(4) Specify a tolerable misstatement for this population. Include any considerations that were used in arriving at this parameter.

(5) Specify a point estimate of the population misstatement. Describe the method by which this determination was made.

(6) Calculate the appropriate sample size. Show the formula being used and identify each element within this formula.

Exhibit 12-5

Abernethy and Chapman

SAMPLING FOR VARIABLES - DIFFERENCE ESTIMATION

Client: _____

Form Completed By: _____

Audit Area: _____

Date of Testing: _____ Year Ending: _____

(1) State the objectives of the audit testing and define misstatement conditions:

(2) Define the population:

(3) Define the sampling unit:

(4) Specify the acceptable level of risk for incorrect acceptance and identify the confidence coefficient (Z value) for this percentage:

(5) Specify the acceptable level of risk for incorrect rejection and identify the confidence coefficient (Z value) for this percentage:

(6) Specify a tolerable misstatement for this population:

(7) Specify a point estimate of the population misstatement:

(8) Compute appropriate sample size (all computations should be attached):

(9) Indicate the method used to draw a random sample:

(10) Recompute the standard deviation using the entire sample selected:

(11) Calculate the average difference within the sample and extend this figure to the entire population:

(12) Determine the precision interval. Show the formula being used and identify each element within this formula (all computations should be attached):

(13) Identify the upper and lower confidence limits of the population based on the precision interval and the average difference of the sample:

(14) Indicate whether the upper and lower confidence limits lie entirely within the tolerable error parameters:

(15) Recommendations:

CASE 13

ADVISORY SERVICES

Approximately three weeks after completing the 1994 examination of Lakeside Company's financial statements, the CPA firm of Abernethy and Chapman furnished the client's management and board of directors with a letter outlining improvements recommended in the control structure. Deficiencies noted by the audit team were described along with proposed changes in the design of Lakeside's systems and the various control procedures being utilized. The firm provides this type of report as a service to each of its audit clients.

Abernethy and Chapman cited at several points in this letter the need to further automate the gathering and reporting of information within the organization. According to the auditors, a large percentage of the data generated by Lakeside has to be hand-recorded onto preprinted forms and then physically routed to the various parties needing the information. Although these procedures had proven adequate when the company was comprised of only 2 or 3 stores, recent growth had placed a serious strain on the systems' ability to operate effectively. Errors and lost forms were not uncommon; a number of instances had been encountered during the audit where shipments were delayed, incorrect inventory was acquired, and payments were misrecorded. Service to the company's customers appeared to be hampered by Lakeside's inability to disseminate information quickly and efficiently.

Shortly after receiving this report, Benjamin Rogers, Lakeside's president, telephoned Dan Cline, the audit partner with Abernethy and Chapman. Rogers expressed considerable interest in correcting these deficiencies. He commented that future corporate growth depended on Lakeside's commitment to "move into the 21st century so that our customers receive the outstanding service that will make them want to buy from us again and again." Following this conversation, Cline asked David Klontz, an advisory services partner with the CPA firm, to contact Rogers and outline the types of technical assistance offered by Abernethy and Chapman. Cline wanted Rogers to know that specialized skills were available within the firm to implement the desired changes in Lakeside's organization.

Klontz arranged a luncheon meeting with Rogers in order to describe the range of services provided by the firm. During their discussion, Klontz recommended that, as a first step, Lakeside should expand its use of computers to include terminals at strategic points within the operation. Additional software programs could then be purchased or developed to perform specified operating tasks for the company. In response, Rogers admitted to possessing little knowledge of computer applications. He had previously resisted the expansion of its computer facilities because of the enormous difficulties he foresaw in converting to a fully automated data processing system. Selecting a new computer, acquiring software, and installing new systems seemed an almost overwhelming chore to Rogers. Just as importantly, he could only envision a few ways in which an enhanced computer system would be adapted to the specific needs of the Lakeside Company. "In the past, I have been very hesitant. I have never understood how the benefits of further computerization could possibly outweigh the many problems and costs involved. However, our growth seems to require that I make changes in the way that I think."

Klontz assured Rogers that the CPA firm would be pleased to investigate Lakeside's needs in detail and then recommend the purchase of a specific computer system. Thereafter, personnel from Abernethy and Chapman would either develop appropriate software for the company or identify outside computer programs to be acquired. The firm was also willing to assist in the installation of all new systems as well as the training of Lakeside employees. According to Klontz, this entire process would create little disturbance within Lakeside's organization. After posing a number of questions about computers and accounting systems, Rogers requested that Klontz prepare a complete proposal to describe possible future actions.

Following this luncheon, Klontz reviewed the entire Lakeside work paper file maintained by Abernethy and Chapman. He studied the design of each of the systems that had been analyzed by the audit team. With this understanding of the client's organization and current control structure, he began to write descriptions of the various functions that could be further automated. The first portion of this list is reproduced in Exhibit 13-1. When completed, Klontz will present these ideas to Rogers as a basis for determining the specific activities that a newly-acquired computer system would be designed to accomplish.

DISCUSSION QUESTIONS

(1) During the audit, Abernethy and Chapman apparently uncovered a number of control problems within Lakeside's organization. What action should have been taken if the audit team had discovered a material weakness in the client's control structure?

(2) Small organizations may, over time, grow into large companies. At what point does the conversion to an automated system become appropriate?

(3) Rogers admits to being hesitant about acquiring and converting to a fully automated accounting system. Considering the prevalence of computers in today's world, why would a business person be so troubled by this action?

(4) Why has the offering of advisory services become so commonplace in public accounting firms?

(5) If Lakeside does convert to a completely-computerized system, how does this change impact on the audit work performed by Abernethy and Chapman in subsequent examinations?

(6) After completing the annual audit, Abernethy and Chapman proposed that the client develop new accounting systems. Thereafter, technical assistance was offered to the client in establishing these same systems. Thus, the firm is in a position to generate revenues as a result of its own recommendations. Does this action constitute a conflict of interests?

(7) The public accounting profession is frequently criticized for allowing firms to provide advisory services to audit clients. The assertion is made that independence is lost in two ways by offering such assistance. First, the auditor gains a vested interest in the client since future financial success is a reflection of the wisdom of the firm's advice. Second, the accounting systems being examined in future years will have been developed or recommended by the auditor's own organization. In both instances, the appearance as well as the actual existence of independence is said to be eroded by the firm's dual role. Does providing advisory services to clients threaten the public's faith in the independent auditing profession? Can these services affect the way that the auditor views the relationship with the client?

WRITTEN QUESTIONS

(1) In Exhibit 13-1, Klontz has begun to describe the functions that could be automated by Lakeside. Using the information provided in the previous 12 cases, complete this memorandum.

(2) In a computerized accounting system, the question of maintaining adequate control becomes an important issue because traditional control procedures are not always applicable. Using the functions determined in written question (1), describe the control features that should be designed into the client's system.

LIBRARY ASSIGNMENT

(1) Read the following as well as any other published information concerning the independence of an auditor that also does consulting work:

"CPAs as Consultants: Conflict of Interest?" United States Banker, November, 1991, p. 23.

"The Effect on Independence when a CPA has a Financial Interest in a Client or Participates in a Client's Decision Making," Journal of Accountancy, September, 1987, p. 112.

"Auditor Performance of MAS: A Study of Its Effects on Decisions and Perceptions," Accounting Horizons, June, 1988, p. 31.

"CPA Consulting Services: A New Standard," Ohio CPA Journal, June, 1992, p. 43.

"Nonaudit Services: How Much is Too Much?" Journal of Accountancy, December, 1980, p. 51.

In this case, the firm of Abernethy and Chapman was asked to do consulting work for Lakeside that is completely separate and unrelated to the audit of the financial statements. Write a report discussing the potential conflict of interest when an auditor does consulting work for an audit client. Does this relationship cause the independence of the auditor to be violated? Why or why not?

Exhibit 13-1

Abernethy and Chapman

FUNCTIONS TO BE COMPUTERIZED
LAKESIDE COMPANY

Memo Prepared by: David Klontz

(1) Telephone Sales

Telephone orders are received by an operator in the sales department. Pertinent information for each transaction is entered directly into a computer terminal: client name and address, account number, and the quantity and serial numbers of the items being acquired. The computer verifies the client data against an approved customer file. The specific purchases are then compared to a list of inventory items currently being held in the company's warehouse. The computer indicates to the operator the validity of the client's credit and the availability of the inventory. This information is conveyed immediately over the telephone to the customer with the transaction finalized at that time. The operator either enters approval for the sale or voids the transaction.

(2) Inventory Shipments

The computer maintains a list of valid sales transactions in chronological order. Using a terminal, the shipping department requests the next order to be processed. The customer and address are shown on the screen as well as the individual items that have been acquired. Once this merchandise has been packed, the department enters the date of the shipment, the bill of lading number, and the specific inventory being transferred. The computer verifies the shipment data against the order and indicates any items that do not match.